Praise for Salim Mansur's *Delectable Lie*:

"Clear thinkers are rare, and so are powerful polemicists. Courageous human beings are rarer still, but the rarest of all is to find the three combined in one person. Meet Salim Mansur." – George Jonas

"A brilliant academic and thought-provoking journalist, Salim Mansur explains what liberal democracy really means, and why the protection of individual rights that lies at its heart is under constant assault from the 'group think' mentality of state-imposed multiculturalism." – Lorrie Goldstein, Senior Associate Editor, *Toronto Sun*

"Professor Salim Mansur is a man of exceptional courage, powerful insight, and possessed of both a delightful and energetic prose style" – Rex Murphy, "The Point of View" on CBC *The National*, and host of CBC Radio One, *Cross Country Checkup*

"In an age of ideological conformity such as ours, it takes courage to speak against the prevailing orthodoxy. This is a courageous book. Professor Mansur exposes how multiculturalism corrodes the values and traditions that sustain Canada as a liberal democratic order. The result is a book to galvanize Canadians against the apostles of extremist progressivism." – Robert Sibley, *Ottawa Citizen* and adjunct professor in political science at Carleton University

"Salim Mansur has the courage to state clearly and openly what many have chosen to ignore: that the multiculturalism project is flawed at its very core. We would all benefit in reading him carefully." – Richard Bastien, editor-in-chief of the *Canadian Observer*

"Canada led the Western world into the multicultural mire in 1988, ironically under a Conservative government. Salim Mansur's deep and scintillating analysis should help the country out of this illiberal and unfortunate policy." – Daniel Pipes, PhD, president of the Middle East Forum and Taube distinguished fellow at the Hoover Institution of Stanford University

"Don't wait for the movie. All the elements needed to entertain and instruct are already present in Mansur's book: incisive rendering, a great 'plot,' a host of interesting 'characters,' sharp ideas and important revelations. Only the book can do justice to itself. Salim Mansur is one of the few, reliable go-to Muslim scholars in the field of Islamic studies." – David Solway, essayist and author of 20 books including *Chess Pieces* and *The Big Lie: On Terror, Antisemitism and Identity*

"As a Muslim exponent of freedom and democracy who immigrated to Canada from war-torn South Asia in 1974, Prof. Salim Mansur is uniquely well qualified to evaluate multiculturalism. Western policy makers would do well to heed his timely warning that this misguided policy could lead over time 'to the unravelling of a liberal democracy, such as Canada, and the ultimate meltdown of its own historically evolved identity.'" – Rory Leishman, author of *Against Judicial Activism: The Decline of Freedom and Democracy in Canada*

"With this important book, Professor Mansur, himself an immigrant to Canada ('a brown guy' as he puts it), has fired a daring and resounding shot across the bow of the Canadian ship of public opinion by explaining, in crystal clear prose, why multicultural policy has brought discord instead of unity to our once-peaceable kingdom. Public debate over a whole range of official orthodoxies has been increasingly impoverished in recent decades, and we can only hope that this book, so unafraid and stimulating, will plant us firmly on the road back to the open society we once enjoyed." – W.D. Gairdner, author of *The Trouble with Canada...Still!*

"Salim Mansur presents a devastating critique of multiculturalism that is unusual in two big ways. The first is that he is surprisingly sympathetic with many of the intentions behind it, and charitable even when he cannot be sympathetic. The second is the way he goes beyond the conventions and platitudes of a 'policy wonk' survey, with sharp, organizing insights of the kind we might expect from a fine historian, or even novelist. He does not merely analyse. He has lived the implications of 'multicultural policy,' and he has looked people who have experienced real dislocation, in the eye. He has thought and felt his way into radically 'other' points of view. There is a sincerity and genuineness in his account that holds one's attention, and makes one care." – David Warren, *Ottawa Citizen*

DELECTABLE LIE:
a liberal repudiation of multiculturalism

by

Salim Mansur

Published by

Mantua Books

Brantford Ontario N3T 6J9

www.mantuabooks.com

Library and Archives Canada Cataloguing in Publication

Mansur, Salim
   Delectable lie : a liberal repudiation of multiculturalism / Salim Mansur.

ISBN 978-0-9869414-0-5

   1. Multiculturalism. 2. Multiculturalism--Political aspects.
3. Multiculturalism--Canada. I. Title.

HM1271.M35 2011   305.8   C2011-905354-3

Copyright Salim Mansur 2011

Cover art by S.H. Rotberg

The publisher acknowledges, with thanks, the assistance of the International Free
Press Society – Canada.

for Ben Singer,
respected colleague and dear friend

Contents

Introduction

DELECTABLE LIE

The origin of freedom lies in breathing.
— Elias Canetti,
Nobel Prize in Literature 1981

Freedom is readily understood by most people, and especially by people confined to dwell under conditions where their own wishes on how to live their lives and speak their thoughts are constrained. There should be no mystery about what freedom is, and what it means. It is as simple and necessary as breathing is to living. Though philosophers and theologians have discussed the matter in their learned roles, people individually and collectively know instinctively when they are unable to live freely. History begins, it might be said, with the quest for freedom. It is as ancient as when Moses led his people, the Jews, from exile under the oppressive rule of the Pharaoh in Egypt into freedom, and as recent as the dismantling of the Berlin Wall in November 1989 that marked the end of communist rule in divided Europe. The universal thirst for freedom — symbolized, for instance, in the iconic image of the solitary individual standing unarmed in front of advancing tanks during the 1989 Tiananmen Square protests in Beijing, China, or in the story of the self-immolation by a despairing and humiliated fruit-seller, Mohammed Bouazizi, that sparked an uprising in his native Tunisia against dictatorship and heralded the Arab Spring of 2011 for freedom against despotic rule in countries of the Middle East and North Africa — is a commonly understood language across cultures.

And yet freedom remains a contested idea among individuals and in society. Its quest has been regularly frustrated by the more immediate needs or *equality* in society. The demand for equality as a remedy for history's injustices is irresistible in all societies, and has been the motive force for reform and revolution. This is increasingly so in the age of democracy, as is ours. The idea of equality being hugely potent, it frequently trumps the idea of freedom in the march of history.

In our time the ideology of *multiculturalism* — the set of ideas that all cultures are equal and deserving of equal treatment in a liberal democracy such as Canada — is linked to the pressing demand for equality in Western societies as these become increasingly *multi-ethnic* due to immigration and open borders.

When first proposed, the idea of an "official" multiculturalism program to be sponsored by the state, supported by taxpayers, and monitored and enforced by thought-police (human rights commissions) was at best dubious, and at worst is by its very nature poised against Western liberalism. Moreover, as mentioned, it was based on the false idea — another official lie, really — that all cultures are equal. However, that is an orthodoxy of the last century increasingly dismissed by serious thinkers. That is because there are established criteria making it possible to judge the achievements of all cultures, whether in the arts and literature, religion, philosophy, technology, modes of governance, or science; but the primary criterion that makes possible all human achievement is freedom.

My point is that although multiculturalism once seemed a very good idea, at least to politicians and others smitten with the ambition for unity, it is increasingly shown to be a lie — a *delectable lie*, perhaps, yet a lie nevertheless — that is *destructive of the West's liberal democratic heritage, tradition, and values based on individual rights and freedoms*. This could have been foretold, as indeed those philosophers and historians of ideas who viewed freedom as immeasurably more important than equality in the development of the West did foretell. They admonished people against the temptation to abridge freedom in pursuit of equality.

In modern history the dilemma — the clash — between freedom (or liberty) and equality was posed starkly in the French Revolution with the revolutionary slogan "Liberty, Equality, Fraternity." Liberty and equality were now to be linked, and in the very linkage of these words, liberty was mentioned first because it was to precede equality in importance. However, because any notion of equality that aims at social and economic levelling always behaves as a universal solvent, this linkage began to reverse itself. The result was that equality was soon to trump liberty in the Western world. As so many important thinkers of the past two or three centuries have been at such great pains to warn us, the dilemmas and perils that will always erupt in any revolutions that privilege equality over liberty are doomed eventually to vanquish the latter.

The temptation for equality, as revolutions by decree make all men equal, comes with the price of denuding man of his freedom and turning him into another cog in the collectivist machine. In *Reflections on History*, Jacob Burckhardt writes the consideration of history begins with "the one point accessible to us, the one eternal center of all things — man, suffering, striving, doing, as he is and was and ever shall be" (1979: 34). From this perspective man is both the agent and subject of politics and history. His freedom — the extent to which he can act as he wishes without any external coercion save his own prudence and desires — is the positive measure of how open and supportive a culture is in terms of individual freedom. And in this respect the West, culturally speaking, stands distinctly apart from all other cultures and civilizations in the past and present.

Freedom is fragile and man's wish to be free (*freedom* must not be confused with *licentiousness* as is often done mistakenly or deliberately) is undermined by ideas that mobilize the collective against the individual. In our world in the early years of the twenty-first century freedom remains more or less confined to one part of the world even as most people everywhere desire it. Only in the West — that is countries of Western Europe, the United States, Canada, Australia and New Zealand — and in Israel, we find people enjoy freedom as individual rights, and any curtailment of these protected rights may only occur in accordance with constitutional requirements. But since freedom is the distinguishing feature of the West, the assault on freedom has been ferocious in the West as were those mounted by the twin forces of totalitarianism — fascism, or Nazism, and Soviet Communism — in the last century. In the new century the West is confronted with a new, or third, challenge of totalitarianism in the form of Islamism and its asymmetrical assault on liberal democracy increasingly since the terrorist attacks of September 11, 2001 against the United States.

Albert Camus used the metaphor of a virus that spreads infectious disease to describe the assault of totalitarianism on freedom in his novel *The Plague*. The scourge of plague might be contained, even temporarily defeated, with much effort and at great cost. But it cannot be entirely eliminated. Camus concluded his fictional narrative of the plague that nearly destroyed the town of Oran, Algeria, sometime in 194- (the setting and time to be read for the defeat of France by Nazi Germany in the Second World War) with a warning. He wrote that "the plague bacillus never dies or vanishes entirely, that it can remain dormant for dozens of years in furniture or clothing, that it waits patiently in bedrooms, cellars, trunks, handkerchiefs and old papers, and that perhaps the day will come when, for the instruction or misfortune of mankind, the plague will rouse its rats and send them to die in some well-contented city" (2002: 237-8). In other words freedom advances, however slowly and uncertainly, by holding back with much effort the forces opposed to freedom that never concede defeat in their effort to weaken and extinguish it.

The assault of multiculturalism on liberal democracy is indirect and self-inflicted. It comes in the form of addiction to the pleasing notion that multiculturalism enriches liberal democracy. This deprecates the consequence that liberal democracy's core principle of individual freedom is undermined by extending recognition to groups defined through collective identity opposed culturally to it. As immigration changes the demographic profile of a liberal democracy such as Canada, multiculturalism empowers immigrants from non-Western societies to demand that their host country adapt to the cultural requirements of immigrants instead of the other way around. Multiculturalism is the slippery slope upon which Canada has positioned itself as a liberal democracy, and if the ride continues unchecked the end then is predictable. This book is an unvarnished look into multiculturalism as a delectable lie that imperils Canada as it does other liberal democracies in the West.

≈≈

Sometime in the mid-1990s, when Pierre Trudeau made a rare visit to the Parliament in Ottawa, the speaker of the House of Commons arranged for a private luncheon attended by a dozen selectively invited Liberal members. Each guest was given the opportunity to pose one question to the former prime minister. Chris Cobb, writing in the *Ottawa Citizen* nearly a decade later, recalled the exchange between Trudeau and invited guests as some of those present recollected it. After several relatively routine questions, former Liberal MP John Bryden remembered asking Trudeau about the multiculturalism policy his government introduced in the early 1970s. In Cobb's retelling, Bryden asked,

"Mr. Trudeau, you were one of the key architects of multiculturalism and now we are in a situation where many newcomers to Canada consider their ethnicity before being Canadian. Is this the outcome you wanted?"

There was silence around the table as the former prime minister thought before replying: "No, this is not what I wanted."

According to Mr. Bryden, Mr. Trudeau made no attempt to hide his disappointment that Canada and the federal presence had all but disappeared in Quebec.

"It was fascinating to hear," said Mr. Bryden. "It was clear that he was deeply disappointed that under the Mulroney government and driven by a fear of separatism, the whole multiculturalism policy had been *twisted to celebrate a newcomer's country of origin and not a celebration of the newcomer becoming part of the Canadian fabric*" (italics added).[1]

I am not quite certain if it is proper to infer from the measured response of the prime minister who initiated multiculturalism as a policy for Canada that he had come very close to renouncing the same. Trudeau died a year before the terrorist attacks in New York City and Washington on September 11, 2001, that opened a new period in world politics — the "clash of civilizations" — of which Samuel Huntington, a distinguished professor of political science at Harvard, had warned (Huntington 1996). Doubts about multiculturalism, as

---

[1] C. Cobb, "Canada's lost promise of multiculturalism," *Ottawa Citizen*, July 4, 2005.

Trudeau expressed, and warnings about a new and troubling period in world politics following the end of the Cold War and the disintegration of Soviet Union in 1991, compel us to reconsider the appropriateness of multiculturalism as a set of ideas and policies within a liberal democratic country such as Canada some forty years on.

The world at the end of the first decade of the twenty-first century is much different from the world at the end of the 1960s, as the promises of the earlier times have been severely shaken. The same is true about politics in Canada: the cheerful optimism of the centenary year has been jolted by the politics of separatism in Quebec, by the demographic changes through immigration in the main urban centres, by the forces of globalization and free trade agreements, and by the insidious nature of security threats from international terrorism — in particular, radical Islam or Islamism — to an open, liberal, democratic society. To those forces were added the economic uncertainties of a global recession that came quite unannounced in the late summer of 2008.

When Trudeau initiated multiculturalism as a federal policy, Canada was still basking in the glow of the centennial celebrations, even though the "strains of affluence," in the words of historian Desmond Morton were being felt across the breadth of the country (Morton 2000). The strains Morton described resulted from the pressures of the transition from the old Dominion of Canada to the broadly felt need by Canadians, as they celebrated their country's centenary, to become a self-assured modern state with an increasing global presence of its own. The arrangements of old Canada were felt to be too constrictive to meet the demands of new Canada that had begun to emerge following the end of the Second World War.

Canada had risen to new prominence as an important ally and contributor to the winning of that war. And as Canadian soldiers returned home from fighting abroad, they found a new urban Canada in the making with the country shifting from an agricultural to an industrial economy. In Quebec the transition from the old to the new became so marked in every aspect of the economy, politics, and culture of the province that the changes came to be referred to as the Quiet Revolution. Quebec's awakening, beginning in the first half of the past century, to the demands of a modern society, and the evolving effort by the French-speaking majority to attain independent statehood, would be the most serious internal challenge pushing the old Dominion to remake itself into the new Canada. Yet these internal strains paled in comparison to events in the United States and Europe; Canada, in contrast to the world outside, appeared as a peaceful, orderly, and stable democracy of much civility.

In the United States, the anti-Vietnam War movement joined with the civil rights movement in 1967 to gravely undermine public authority. In 1968, these movements came to a head when anti-war protests forced President Lyndon Johnson to abandon seeking a second-term in the White House; and civil rights protests turned violent following the murder of Martin Luther King, Jr. In Europe, discontent with the existing political order burst out with student rebellion in the streets of Paris in May 1968. The generation of 1968 had come of age in the two decades after the end of the Second World War riding the most profound technological, economic, and social changes in world history. A decade earlier, in 1957, the Soviet Union had put a satellite into orbit around the earth, signalling that the rivalry among nation-states, especially the great powers, would be exported into space. The Soviet challenge was picked up by the United States and in 1969 an American, Neil Armstrong, descended from his spacecraft on to the surface of the moon. From the perspective of man on the moon, the earth appeared as a fragile planet on which the political arrogance of the human species to fence it off with national boundaries made no sense. For students in Europe and North America in rebellion against authority, the spirit of the time went beyond questioning the existing dominant political arrangements. Instead, for them John Lennon's song *Imagine* with its lyrics — "Imagine there's no countries…And no religion too," — became a sort of anthem.

The depth and speed of change people felt at the end of the 1960s were just about unprecedented. The best-selling sociologist Alvin Toffler captured the sense of this hurtling locomotive of change in his hugely successful book *Future Shock* (1970). Change can be both exhilarating and discomforting. For those caught in the accelerating transition from the old certainties of the past to the new uncertainties of the future, there would also be alienation from society, most acutely felt by the student generation of 1968. Around this time, two of Canada's greatly respected academic scholars, one a philosopher and the other a literary critic, George Grant and Northrop Frye, drew attention to how their country was being affected by events and things in ways that meant, for better or worse, the demise of the old order.

In 1965 Grant published a little book, *Lament for a Nation*, in which he expressed himself somewhat "angrily" about the passing of English-Canadian nationalism as the country was being drawn into a tighter embrace of American capitalism. He wrote, "Those who loved the older traditions of Canada may be allowed to lament what has been lost, even though they do not know whether or not that loss will lead to some greater political good" (Grant: 96). In 1967, Canada's centennial year, Frye was invited to give the Whidden Lectures at McMaster University in Hamilton, Ontario, and he chose for his lectures the theme "The Modern Century" (later published as a book with the theme as title) to reflect on the period of history during which Canada came of age. Frye contemplated the journey the world had made during Canada's century from 1867 to 1967 in terms of discoveries made in science, advances in technology, and creativity in arts and literature and the cumulative unintended effect of these changes on the human condition in terms of breeding anxiety and alienation. He observed that alienation arose from the "sense that man has lost control, if he ever had it, over his own destiny" (Frye: 24). Alienation from the existing order of things paradoxically also fuelled the desire for change as it was felt by the 1968 generation. And so the political realm in Canada was primed for change. But, as Frye looked around and took the measure of his country, he commented, "The loss of faith in such a world is centrally a religious problem, but it has a political dimension as well, and one which includes the question we have been revolving around all through: what is it, in society, to which we really owe loyalty?" (121).

Frye's question was aptly phrased. It struck at the heart of the matter, politically speaking, for a generation caught in the crosscurrents of change. For the past few centuries, as European ideas were transported across the ocean to North America, political loyalty was demanded by, and belonged to, the territorially demarcated nation-states that emerged in the seventeenth century. In the second half of the twentieth century, a new idea, the "global village," found expression. The man credited with the coining of this expression was a Canadian, Marshall McLuhan, professor of English literature and communication theorist at the University of Toronto. Though the expression at its origin had a negative connotation, by the end of the

1960s the idea of the "global village" captured the mood of the time. The world was shrinking in terms of distance, given rapid developments in the means of transportation and communication, and in this shrunken world, as the older arrangements of nation-states in Europe and North America were being skeptically re-examined, Frye's question of where, how, and to whom people owed loyalty in a global village became moot.

In retrospect, the latter half of the past century was the second "golden age" of liberal capitalism in the modern history of the West. The first "golden age" was the period between the Congress of Vienna in 1815 and the outbreak of the First World War in 1914. During the five decades following the Second World War, liberal capitalism in the West went through renewal, innovation, and strains of affluence and expansion as it spurred globalization, eventually beating off the challenge posed by communism. No society in human history had ever been as productive and rich as the West became in this second "golden age" of liberal capitalism. The West's success in raising the standard of living of its citizens was matched by the expansion of freedom for individuals in society recognized as fundamental human rights to be respected and protected by authorities. Canada, as an integral part of the West, contributed to and benefited from the success of liberal capitalism during this period. And the growth of the Canadian economy made it possible to smooth the rough edges of liberal capitalism — to respond to the strains of affluence — through the introduction of social welfare benefits and universal health care as common goods for the whole society.

More difficult, however, was how to respond to the strain on the idea of nationhood that was unsettling Canadians. Indeed, Canada's situation was rather unusual among the Western liberal democracies. As English-speaking Canadians began to feel uneasy about state-promoted nationalism — and in this respect they were at one with Europeans troubled by their own violent history — French-speaking Quebecers began to respond positively to nationalism that sought at a minimum a revision of the existing powers of Confederation. It was under these circumstances that the Liberal government of Prime Minister Lester Pearson announced the making of the Royal Commission on Bilingualism and Biculturalism in 1963. Pearson's B & B Commission (as it came to be called) was launched, according to the historian Kenneth McNaught, in response to the "deepening crisis of French-Canadian aspirations, and of Anglophone reluctance to contemplate substantial changes of policy" that would affect the federal arrangements; and the task set for the Commission was "to document the sources of the crisis and to suggest paths to a federal future of equality between the 'two founding races'" (McNaught: 308). It was from the labours of the B & B Commission that the idea of multiculturalism as a policy for Canada was born in the new Liberal government of Prime Minister Pierre Trudeau after he won majority power in the 1968 election. Since then, multiculturalism has spread to other liberal democracies of the West, including Australia.

≈≈

Though the official policy of multiculturalism as set forth by Ottawa was initially well received, in time critics from both the left and the right of the political spectrum seemed to agree that it was setting ethnic groups apart rather than bringing them closer in the building of a more cohesive national identity. Among the critics on the left, one of the most prominent voices was that of Neil Bissoondath, an immigrant from Trinidad, whose book *Selling Illusions: The Cult of Multiculturalism in Canada* (1994) was a hard-hitting inquiry into the reality of what multiculturalism actually meant in the lives of Canadians. On the right were voices such as that of William Gairdner, author of *The Trouble with Canada* (1990), who was concerned about how multiculturalism was diminishing the traditional conservative values of the majority European population that built Canada.

In this study my main concern is with some of the unintended consequences of multiculturalism that are weakening the basic principles of a liberal democracy, such as Canada. The events of September 11, 2001 showed, I believe, how multiculturalism has become an instrument of extremist political ideology, such as Islamism, and can work against the values and interests of liberal democracies. In chapter one I trace the adoption of multiculturalism as official policy in Canada, and the effort that followed of constructing a theoretical foundation for the policy. In chapter two I examine the meaning of multiculturalism in terms of identity politics, and in chapter three I discuss the related topics of immigration and citizenship. The place and role of history in democracy, and what this means for multiculturalism is the focus of chapter four; in chapter five I look at how multiculturalism subverts freedom through censorship and constraints placed on freedom of speech by governments and their agencies. In chapters six and seven I analyze multiculturalism in the context of the terrorist attacks on America, and in terms of the effect on the West of open-door immigration. I am a skeptic of multiculturalism as an official state-directed policy, but I am realist enough to recognize that this official policy will not be reversed or dismantled, as it has become deeply entrenched in the politics of Canada and other Western democracies. But I do believe there is room for constraining any further growth of multiculturalism at the expense of the liberal values of freedom and individual rights. Though this essay is neither exhaustive nor pretends to be, yet hopefully it will be rewarding if readers find the liberal critique of multiculturalism offered here has highlighted a vital problem, and that defending liberalism in our world where it is under siege from the assault of collectivist politics of both the left and the right is seen as an urgent cause.

≈≈

Since my critique of multiculturalism is from a small-l *liberal* perspective distinct from the animating spirit of the contemporary Liberalism with a big-L of the Liberal party in Canada or Britain, a few words here on what I mean by *liberalism* will be useful. My education and thinking on the subject of liberalism have been influenced by the writings of Friedrich Hayek, Karl Popper, John Stuart Mill, and Isaiah Berlin. In their work, *liberalism* is about liberty, about the freedom of the individual from any untoward coercion by the collective in society, and can be traced back "to the theme of the links between the rights to personal property and individual liberty" that first found expression in John Locke's writing in the seventeenth century (Gray: 14). Locke's theme would be refined and advanced later in the works of Montesquieu, Adam Smith, David

Hume, and others, and it would be carried with other ideas of the Enlightenment through the eighteenth into the nineteenth century in what John Gray calls "the liberal era". For Hayek, *liberalism* as an idea meant, he recalled, how Lord Acton always used "'liberal' in its true and comprehensive sense,... one to whom individual liberty is of supreme value and 'not a means to a higher political end'" (Hayek 1992: 209). This meaning of *liberalism* might now best be referred to as *classical liberalism*, or *classical liberty*, with its emphasis on individual freedom in a society ruled by law.

Implicit in classical liberalism is the belief that all men are created equal and deserving of equal treatment under the law. But towards the end of the nineteenth century, another strain of liberalism emerged with emphasis on equality. The social liberals argued that for a truly equitable society to emerge it was necessary for the state to treat different groups of people differently. This would be the slippery slope for the argument to expand the powers of the state over the people, and to make the case that experts in the various social sciences possessed knowledge and insight on how to create a social order that would be more equitable and just than the social order that worked on the basis of the "invisible hand" of markets organized voluntarily and spontaneously by free individuals coming together of their own accord. It meant for social liberals that, if equality required attenuating freedom, then the state should not be inhibited in its quest to favour equality over freedom. Increasingly in the twentieth century, therefore, social liberals moved to embrace some variant of socialism and succeeded in engineering a social welfare state that is intrusive in the lives of individuals in return for state-provided benefits. *My* use of the terms *liberal* and *liberalism* refers to *classical* liberalism. And this reference to classical liberalism, as Hayek notes in his essay "Why I am not a Conservative" appended to his great work *The Constitution of Liberty*, is related to "the fact that the belief in integral freedom is based on an essentially forward-looking attitude and not on any nostalgic longing for the past or a romantic admiration for what has been" (2006: 354).

Chapter One

WHY DID CANADA TURN AGAINST ITSELF?

In July 2007 Canada marked the one hundred and fortieth anniversary of its founding. The Canadian story is a remarkable one of unbroken democratic government and the rule of law, of being one of the oldest functioning democracies after Britain, the Netherlands and the United States. In the words of Canada's twenty-sixth Governor-General, Adrienne Clarkson, "Our Constitution is one of the oldest in the world: the French have had five in the time that we've had ours."[2] Yet Canadians suffer from endless soul-searching over how to define Canadian identity that foreigners find baffling. This effort stretches back over the life of Canada and continues ceaselessly into our time. It could be said this search for Canadian *identity* is in itself a defining characteristic of being Canadian. From Hugh MacLennan's *Two Solitudes* to Andrew Cohen's *The Unfinished Canadian*, from Lord Durham's often quoted observation from his 1838 Report that he "found two nations warring in the bosom of a single state" to the passage 150 years later in July 1988 of the Canadian Multiculturalism Act recognizing in law "the cultural and racial diversity of Canadian society," the Canadian story also appears to be one never-ending quest for self-definition. This quest is possibly indicative of why in a country of immigrants the subject of national identity remains fluid

---

[2] A. Clarkson, "Understanding our democracy," *National Post* (Toronto), May 26, 2009, p. A18.

and elusive in the absence of an over-arching common belief or myth that the people hold dear making of them into one nation.

An overview of Canada's history since 1867 tells us, on the other hand, the vast geography that describes the country has its own enduring pull upon immigrants who arrive, and despite the manifold differences among them of languages and cultures assimilate them into becoming *Canadian* irrespective of the confusion surrounding the idea of Canadian identity. In some respect this confusion is an aspect of Canada's transition from a *modern* to a *post-modern* state, or from a "demanding" state that imposes an identity on the people to an "accommodating" state disinclined to insist on a state-constructed identity for the people and, instead, accepting or celebrating their ethnic diversity. A modern state is itself a relatively recent phenomenon in history, distinct from all previous pre-modern societies that were more or less organized within the boundaries of multi-racial empires along cultural lines wherein collective identities based on race and religion were dominant. The birth of the modern state occurs with the dissolution of empires and therein evolves the idea of citizenship based on individual rights taking precedence over collective or group identity, as well as the making of a uniform code of law and institutions of the state. The modern state is more or less "homogenizing" or "assimilative" and, thereby, integrates its people as citizens into one commonly shared identity. In contrast, the post-modern state would be one where the dominant nationalist ideology of the modern state gets disputed, and this dispute signifies the discomfort with the homogenizing or assimilative nature of state-constructed identity for citizens and the need for re-thinking the notion of identity that reflects the ethno-cultural diversity of the people.

Identity is about belonging and association, and the loyalty that such attachment generates in people collectively or individually. Amartya Sen, the 1998 Nobel prize-wining economist, in *Identity and Violence* noted identity rarely is singular and that the normal condition for an individual is to cherish multiple over-lapping identities of belonging to family, ethnic group, religious community, professional associations and state (2006: 18-21). The post-modern state is riddled with competing demands of plural identities seeking recognition informally at the societal level and formally at the legal-institutional level. The struggle of the modern state in responding to such demands, instead of denying them, is indicative of its transition into what might eventually constitute the post-modern state. In looking back over nearly half-century of Canadian politics, the struggle within Canada for accommodating competing identities of immigrants coming together as a people has made of Canada the first of post-modern states adopting *multiculturalism* as her official state identity. This process of advancing and adopting the notion of multiculturalism in Canada has stretched over four decades and since this has provided Canadians with valuable experience in this "officially" adopted experiment, they are well-positioned to critically evaluate what multiculturalism has meant and where their country might be headed as a result.

II.

The terms of reference in appointing the Royal Commission on Bilingualism and Biculturalism by the Pearson government in July 1963 made no mention of multiculturalism. The preliminary report of the commission was delivered to the government in February 1965. In the preamble of the report the commissioners stated, "Canada, without being fully conscious of the fact, is passing through the greatest crisis in its history" (Royal Commission: 13). The source of this crisis was to be found in the Province of Quebec; and in locating its cause, the commissioners wrote, "it would appear from what is happening that the state of affairs established in 1867, and never since seriously challenged, is now for the first time being rejected by the French Canadians of Quebec" (ibid).

The preliminary report was prepared after the ten commissioners travelled extensively across the country visiting large and small communities, and listening to "thousands of their fellow citizens." The term *multiculturalism* appeared briefly in usage by those citizens who were neither English nor French Canadians, and who objected to the "duality concept" of Canada variously expressed in the terms "equal partnership", "two founding races" and "two nations" (ibid: 50). This objection was encountered mostly in the western provinces. The commissioners were reminded of the role played by Canadians who immigrated from Germany, the Ukraine, the Scandinavian countries, Holland, Poland and elsewhere from Europe in settling the West. These Canadians expressed dissatisfaction with the term "New Canadian" to describe them since many of their ancestors settled in the Maritimes or in the Prairies several generations earlier, and many arrived before the making of the Confederation. When asked how they would like to see Canada defined that would be representative equally of them, the answer

[T]hey often gave was "multiculturalism", or, more elaborately, "the Canadian mosaic." They asked: If two cultures are accepted, why not many? Why should Canada not be a country in which a multitude of cultural groups live side by side yet distinct from one another, all contributing to a richly varied society? Certainly, it was stated, the mosaic idea was infinitely preferable to the "melting pot" (ibid: 51).

The commissioners were repeatedly reminded that behind the idea of Canada as "multicultural" or as a "mosaic" was the expressed desire of those using such terms for a strong affirmation of "One Canada." The deeply held feeling for unity despite the cultural or ethnic diversity of Canada was duly noted. The commissioners wrote, "In the complex ethnic situation existing in Canada, the only kind of unity which can reasonably be striven for and achieved is unity in diversity: the harmonious co-operation of all ethnic groups in the Canadian country as a whole" (ibid: 52). But others have wondered if the phrase is an oxymoron.

In reading the preliminary report of the B & B Commission nearly five decades later the one thing that causes little surprise is the extent to which concerns of Canadians then about their country and their identity ring the same all these years later. Despite the many changes that have occurred since the B & B report was released, the private introspection and the public debate on the subject among Canadians have remained just about the same. The commissioners reported concerns among common Canadians wherever they went outside of Quebec with the fear of "Balkanization" and the urgency for the making of a "One Canada" policy by the federal government. People at the hearings spoke out against the notion of "hyphenated-Canadians," against "regionalism" and the uneasiness of moving too much in the direction of the United States and its idea of the "melting-pot." Canadian identity, it was indicated, needed to be different from the United States, and multiculturalism appeared to be the idea that stood as a counterpoint to the American principle of *e pluribus unum* ("out of many, one"). As the commissioners noted, they "received a strong impression that the over-powering presence of the U.S. obscures the sense of national identity and responsibility among Canadians" (ibid: 59). But the urgency at hand for the commissioners was less of conjuring a Canadian identity for a country that was decidedly a work in progress as the centennial decade unfolded, and more of disentangling the Quebec question which posed "the greatest crisis" in Canada's history.

In October 1969 the B & B Commission submitted volume 4 of its final report dealing with immigration, languages and culture. One year earlier in October 1968 the new Liberal government headed by Prime Minister Pierre Trudeau introduced the Official Languages Bill passed into law in 1969. Canada became officially bilingual, and the next step taken by the government in defining the making of a new country in keeping with the recommendations of the B & B Commission was introducing in the federal parliament Canada's Multicultural Policy of 1971. These policies had the support of all parties in the federal legislature, and with Trudeau's view that a "policy of multiculturalism within a bilingual framework commends itself to the government as the most suitable means of assuring the cultural freedom of Canadians" (Palmer: 136). The only prominent voice of political opposition to Multicultural Policy came from Premier Robert Bourassa of Quebec. Bourassa wrote an open letter to Prime Minister Trudeau in *Le Devoir* on November 17, 1971 in which he stated "with the federal government assuming responsibility for all the cultures which are to be found in Canada, Quebec must take on within its own territory the role of prime defender of the French language and culture" (ibid: 152). Notwithstanding Quebec's misgivings with federally directed multiculturalism that would grow, the stage was set for Canada to push forward with the making of Canadian identity as one reflective of the country's increasingly diverse immigrant population. Canada's official policy of multiculturalism was promulgated in tandem with the policy of official bilingualism and the shift in the pattern of immigration from primarily Europe to an open-door policy of accepting immigrants of non-European origin. Taken together multiculturalism and immigration would push Canada in a direction that was not fully discussed in public, was not given much thought by the government and opposition parties as they generally agreed with the recommendations of the B & B Commission, and Canadians in general did not understand how much of their old Dominion would be changed into a new Canada in the years after the centennial celebrations were over.

III.

With the adoption of the Trudeau government's multicultural policy, Canadians embarked on the path of radically remaking Canada even if this fact was not fully comprehended at the time. Many years later how greatly multiculturalism changed the country was conceded by those — as did John Ibbitson in describing the effects of multiculturalism as the "polite revolution" (see Ibbitson) — who experienced the distance Canada moved from the circumstances of its centennial decade to the social and political reality of the country at the beginning of a new century. In effect Canada became the first major democracy to experiment with designing a society on the basis of multiculturalism, and the road it has travelled from the early uncertain meaning of this idea to the full acknowledgment of it as constitutional and legal-institutional reality of the country. The appointment of Adrienne Louise Clarkson as the first Governor-General of non-European (Chinese) origin in 1999 by Prime Minister Jean Chretien, who was then succeeded by Michaëlle Jean of Haitian origin appointed in 2005 by Prime Minister Paul Martin, symbolized at the highest level of the state the distance Canada had come in implementing multiculturalism as official policy.

When Pierre Trudeau stepped forward on the national stage in 1968 he appeared to embody the spirit of the times. The younger Canadians on the cusp of taking over responsibility for their country from the previous generation were thirsting for new meanings and new challenges in their lives. Trudeau's biographers Stephen Clarkson and Christina McCall wrote:

These were the post-war Canadians who had come of age during the boom years, who had achieved higher levels of education in greater numbers than their parents and grandparents, who had travelled farther and more frequently and had been influenced by the huge post-war influx of European immigrants

— the generation that had absorbed some of the wild hopes for a new social order that were emanating from the young in English Canada's two great mentor countries, the United States and the United Kingdom (1991: 97).

Trudeau's intellectual approach to politics appealed to the post-war generation of Canadians whose credo, given expression by the journalist Peter Desbarats, resonated with his peers at the time. Desbarats wrote, "I am part of a generation of Canadians who have grown up without a sense of inferiority" (ibid). This credo exuded confidence drawing upon the recent history of a country that went the distance at much cost in blood and treasure to defeat evil in its modern incarnation of malevolently corrupted race-nationalism in Europe during the first half of the last century.

In the two decades since the end of World War II as Canadians marked their centennial year, the full horror of Nazi Germany was sufficiently disclosed and absorbed by western democracies. German nationalism under Nazi influence became the agent of Hitler's racial program and pushed Europe into the most disastrous war ever in its history. As a result the post-1945 generation in the West recoiled against any sort of cultural or race-based nationalism that might carry the stink of Hitler and Nazism. For this generation the only sort of nationalism acceptable as benign and promoted as "progressive" would be some sort of civic nationalism inclusive of all people irrespective of ethnic differences in a democratic and secular modern state.

Canadians shared the revulsion for the sort of politics that sparked racial madness and swept Europe into a catastrophic war dragging rest of the world into it. But there was also pride over how Canadians made sacrifices in joining others to defeat race-based politics in Europe and Asia. Revulsion and pride mingled together during the centennial celebration, and Canadians were prepared to critically examine the record of inter-racial relationship in their own country. This record was disturbing when examined from the perspective of a new generation of Canadians more open to the world and more receptive to the idea that Canada should be held up as a model of a tolerant, open and democratic society for members of the United Nations. Before this could occur, however, Canadians needed to turn the page on that record, and those wronged, or their progeny, offered apology and some sort of compensation.

"Racism and nativism," as the Canadian historian W. Peter Ward observed, "are among the common consequences of interracial and cultural contact" (1990: x). Confronting this record of inter-racial relationships is politically difficult and psychologically traumatic. But confronting that record was required if Canadians were to build a colour-blind society. The record of Canada's politics, specially on the west coast with Chinese immigrants forced to pay an unusually high head tax to enter the country during the years immediately before and following the making of the confederation, or the Parliament passing the exclusionary act of 1923 directed at the Chinese in limiting Asian immigrants, were illustrative of "racism and nativism" that Patricia Roy documented in *The Oriental Question: Consolidating a White Man's Province*. There was the troubled relationship between "white" Canadians and East Indian migrants who sought entry into Canada from colonial India on the basis of membership in the British Empire, and the memory of the notorious incident in May 1914 when the Japanese-owned ship *Komagata Maru* with 376 passengers of Indian origin, mostly Sikhs, arrived in Vancouver. Canadian authorities refused to allow the passengers on board to disembark, and the ship was forcibly sent back to Hong Kong (Johnston, 1979). The treatment of Japanese-Canadians during the Second World War when they were evacuated from their homes, dispossessed of their property and interned in camps in the interior of British Columbia on orders from the federal government laid bare, according to Ward, "the limits of Canadian liberal democracy" (1990: xiii). Canadian Jews had their history of suffering racial and religious bigotry, of learning in horror and dismay the government denying Canada as refuge to Jews desperately seeking escape from Hitler's program for the Final Solution of European Jewry (Abella and Troper, 1982). This list is a small indication of the inter-racial record that showed Canada's history was not much better than the record of the United States' history as a "melting pot." And then there loomed ever larger the record of the treatment of aboriginal people, the First Nations, by European settlers on the conscience of a new Canada in the making (Friesen, 1997; and Trigger, 1985).

Multiculturalism was not conceived as public policy to redress the past wrongs of the Canadian society. But once adopted it opened the public square for discussing these past wrongs which would then generate its own political dynamics with affected Canadians increasingly made aware of them, and their demands for redress politicians at all levels of government found increasingly difficult to turn down.

The crisis of the Canadian state pushed by Quebec's demands for special arrangements was also aggravated by similar pressures felt in the United States and other West European democracies resulting from the movement of peoples within and across international boundaries, and the demand for reforms to make the state more inclusive, embracing and respectful of its citizens. In Canada, particularly English Canada, the demand for change and reform, however, did not express itself in rage turning violent — except for the relatively "fringe" politics of the FLQ — as it did south of the border. There the civil rights movement of the American "Negroes" for full participation in politics and society without any racial segregation turned violent. The iconic picture from that period in American history was the clenched fist in black glove salute of the two black athletes, Tommie Smith and John Carlos, on the medal stand in the 1968 Mexico City Olympics after winning gold and bronze medals respectively in the 200 metre race. The black salute signified the demand for inclusion in society of people irrespective of colour or any other differences, and it carried more effectively the message of the civil rights movements than the smoke rising from some of the urban centres of the United States caught in the grip of race violence.

The spirit of the age when Trudeau became prime minister was tending in the direction of reform in politics and in re-writing the rules of the existing social arrangements that visualized a colour-blind non-discriminatory society. "Progressive" politics that mainstream parties espoused shared the premise of a society open to non-white immigrants and receptive, if not celebratory, of the differences of race (ethnicity), languages and religions among the people. This sort of "progressive" politics tended to be multicultural, and multiculturalism became a policy embraced and promoted by all federal parties in Ottawa as the new idea in politics in harmony with the post-colonial world and the hopes embodied in the Charter of the United Nations and the Universal Declaration of Human Rights.

Canada was not alone, however, in adopting multiculturalism as public policy and, eventually, as the distinctive, defining and fundamental characteristic of the Canadian society as laid out in the Multiculturalism Act of 1988. Other immigrant countries, notably

Australia and New Zealand, also adopted multiculturalism as public policy to deal with the changing circumstances in terms of immigration and integration of new arrivals of diverse ethnic origins in once pre-dominantly white Caucasian societies (Kymlicka, 2004). But in Canada there was urgency for reform felt domestically due to the special situation of Quebec in the Canadian federation that was absent in the case of Australia and New Zealand. Hence, the push for making Canada officially bilingual, English and French, was balanced by the idea of "official" multiculturalism that would be colour-blind and supportive of immigrant communities, especially recent arrivals of non-European origin, in retaining their cultures while being encouraged to move into mainstream Canada. Explicit in this idea of multiculturalism was the officially sanctioned view that *all cultures are of equal merit and deserving of equal respect.*

In adopting multiculturalism as official policy in October 1971, Trudeau made the following statement in the parliament:

First, resources permitting, the government will seek to assist all Canadian cultural groups that have demonstrated a desire and effort to continue to develop a capacity to grow and contribute to Canada, and a clear need for assistance, the small and weak groups no less than the strong and highly organized. Second, the government will assist members of all cultural groups to overcome cultural barriers to full participation in Canadian society. Third, the government will promote creative encounters and interchange among all Canadian cultural groups in the interest of national unity. Fourth, the government will continue to assist immigrants to acquire at least one of Canada's official languages in order to become full participants in Canadian society (Palmer: 136).

In the decade that followed the federal government allocated $200 million for Trudeau's initiative, and established a multicultural Directorate within the Department of the Secretary of State to oversee and implement it. Multiculturalism became a top-down effort of the Canadian state to set the markers for the rest of the country the direction in which it would be encouraged to evolve; and, as it would have been expected, interest groups emerged shortly as stake-holders to drive from bottom-up Canadian politics along those markers which Trudeau first spelled out. Trudeau and the circle of policy-makers around him in Ottawa conceived of multiculturalism almost entirely as supportive of group identity in cultural terms and group attachments. This marked the beginning of the tilt for Canada as a liberal democratic society to favour group rights as opposed to individual rights, of federal and provincial governments supportive and protective of minority rights defined in terms of group or collective identity when the most vulnerable minority in any society is the individual, and the defining characteristic of liberal democracy has historically meant the support for and protection of liberty in terms of individual rights.

IV.

Between Trudeau's initiative of October 1971 and the passage of the Canadian Multiculturalism Act under Prime Minster Brian Mulroney's Progressive Conservative government in July 1988, Canada became the first western liberal democracy to adopt multiculturalism as the defining characteristic of the country and one of the directive principles for the government to abide by and promote as policy. It meant, according to section 27 of the Constitution Act of 1982 or the Canadian Charter of Rights and Freedoms, that the notion of collective or group identity based on ethnic origin, language, religion and gender inherent in the idea of multiculturalism would have to be taken into account by the parliament and the courts in considering the fundamental rights and freedoms of Canadians as set forth in Part I of the Charter. In less than two decades following Canada's centenary year celebration, the federal government had led a top-down radical reform of the Canadian society by institutionalizing through public policy, statutes and the Charter that would be somewhat incomprehensible to the founding fathers of the confederation and prime ministers from John A. Macdonald to John Diefenbaker. The speed with which multiculturalism was instituted into the fabric of the Canadian government and society ran ahead of public opinion in general, and of any body of clearly articulated general principles or theory as such of multiculturalism to be found anywhere among the advance industrialized democracies of the West.

Since there was no body of prior existing political or social theory setting forth the idea of, and the need for, multiculturalism as there was with arguments for nationalism, liberalism, and socialism as political philosophy, the public policy initiative was driven by the circumstances of societal changes in western democracies during the second half of the last century. These changes were driven mostly by the external factors of the movement of peoples across international borders resulting from wars, end of European colonialism and shift in immigration policy in older immigrant societies — Canada, Australia and the United States — from race-based consideration to point-based merit system of opening immigration to people of non-European ethnic origin. But eventually there would be the need to construct a political-cum-social theory supporting multiculturalism as public policy, and this theory-building would ride the slipstream of the public policy initiative in Ottawa making Canada a pioneering country in this effort.

The proponents of multiculturalism took it as a given that *liberal democracy* is insufficiently open and accommodating of the fast changing new realities of the post-1945 world. But these new realities are effects of "globalization" brought about by the rapidly shrinking time and distance in terms of communication and transportation around the world for the movement of finance capital, goods, ideas, and people across international boundaries. It is obvious these new realities have been experienced more deeply in liberal democracies as open societies than in societies differently arranged politically speaking, and where as a result we find the push for multiculturalism most vigorously advanced by its proponents. As one proponent observes, the need for multiculturalism arises basically in a liberal democracy, and "its advocacy and critique have to relate to existing, functioning liberal democracies" (Modood: 7). However, the objective social reality of multiculturalism in terms of the togetherness or co-existence of many cultures, that is people coming together from different ethnic and religious backgrounds, within a defined political space is not something new that was missing in the political make-up of liberal democracies such as Canada, Australia, and the United States built by immigrants of many different ethnic background living together. Moreover, all empires in history — given the nature of empires — were multicultural as was the Ottoman Empire until its demise following World War I. Many new states in Asia and Africa established as a result of the ending of European colonialism are of ethnically mixed population. India is a striking example of a country functioning as the world's largest democracy where all of the world's major religions are represented, the country is ethnically multicultural with more than twenty languages officially recognized, and the unity of the country hinges upon the acceptance of the country's immense ethno-cultural diversity on the basis of equality as a constitutional principle.

Empires have been the norm in history, and set against this history of several thousand years the rise of the modern state is a very recent phenomenon of some merely three hundred years (Lal, 2004). The history of the modern state is a European story both in its earliest relatively short-lived manifestation as Greek city-states around the fourth century B.C., and then the making of states in the period beginning with the Protestant Reformation in the sixteenth century. Modern states were territorially defined either by geography (the British Isles) or by force of arms of a central authority (France, Spain), and this territory and its population defended as an independent political entity from rival powers. The mutual recognition of states (or the ruling princely authorities) marked the beginning in Europe of the era of states as sovereign actors that eventually became accepted in international politics and law as the norm around the world.

Modern states are homogenizing in ethno-cultural terms of their population; this process is either top-down as the people are assimilated into the religion and language of the ruling authority, or bottom-up as the state is made to reflect the values and interests of a people self-defined as *nation* (Hall and Ikenberry, 1989; Hobsbawm, 1990; Gellner, 1983). The idea of *nation* as a people ethnically identified on the basis of kinship relations or language is as old as human history, since people have formed groups for basic survival either voluntarily or through coercion. Hence group solidarity and group loyalty have been the oldest building block of society, and Ibn Khaldun (1332-1406), the great Arab historian-philosopher from North Africa, made the logic of group or tribal solidarity (*asabiyya*) the foundational principle of his brilliantly conceived study of history as the rise and decline of dynastic kingdoms and empires. But *nation,* as a new term, was pregnant with the demand for its *self-determination* to establish a state wherein it would find freedom for its full and unfettered self-expression (Kedourie, 1990). Gellner offered the view that *nationalism* preceded the idea of nation and willed the nation into existence. According to Gellner,

It is nationalism which engenders nations, and not the other way round. Admittedly, nationalism uses the pre-existing, historically inherited proliferation of cultures or cultural wealth, though it uses them very selectively, and it most often transforms them radically. Dead languages can be revived, traditions invented, quite fictitious pristine purities restored... Nationalism is not what it seems, and above all it is not what it seems to itself. The cultures it claims to defend and revive are often its own inventions, or are modified out of all recognition (1983: 55-56).

The point to note here about *nationalism* and *nation* in the making of modern state is these terms describe collective or group-based identity. The modern state would be, therefore, the incarnation of the nationalist "will" affirming itself in history, of nationalist self-determination consummated through an act of political exertion at whatever cost a nation was willing to bear in order to secure for itself a state.

The rise and spread of the modern states are embedded in the idea of a people's collective will and interest achieving independent political expression and cultural fulfillment. Modern state is the instrument by which a people coming together as nation seek security and independence from others. And as a collective enterprise the modern state logically has been assimilative of individuals into the state-constructed identity of the people. This assimilative process has been uneven varying from state to state, and rigorous or weak depending on the institutional capacity of individual states. Of the rise of the modern state one contemporary political theorist writes:

The 'modernity' of the states which grew in Europe especially during and after the era of absolutist monarchies was based primarily on their enhanced administrative capacity, their unification of territories under single administrative centers, their replacement of older forms of 'indirect rule' (from tax farming to simply delegating authority to feudal nobilities) with an increasingly direct control of and intervention into their disparate territories and populations, their reliance on popular political participation, their capacity to mobilize citizens for warfare, and their assertion of clear boundaries rather than frontiers. A central part of the state formation project involved the 'pacification' of life within the state's boundaries; indeed, the state's exercise of a monopoly of violence – or at least legitimate violence – became a crucial tenet of political theory (Calhoun: 66-67).

This history of process, formation and consolidation in the emergence of modern states is what makes all states irrespective of size, population and resources objectively similar as sovereign political entities. What makes for the difference is the specific history of the people and the internal arrangements of political rule, or what Max Weber described in his seminal essay "Politics as a Vocation" as the inner justification of "legitimate authority" for the functioning of the state (Gerth and Mills: 77-128).

Liberal democracy is one particular type of state in which the modern philosophy of liberalism gives special meaning to the idea and practice of democracy as government elected by and representative of the people. In its European origin the liberal state also meant *secular* state. This was due to the religious battles that transformed Europe during the age of Reformation, and subsequent philosophical-scientific developments resulting from the works of Copernicus, Galileo, Newton and others in the age of Enlightenment (Cassirer, 1951), that led educated Europeans in increasing numbers to hold the view that religion (that is Christianity) should be a matter of private belief. The liberal secular state is one, as Owen Chadwick explained,

in which government exerts no pressure in favour of one religion rather than another religion; a state in which no social or educational pressure is exerted in favour of one religion rather than another religion or no religion; a state wholly detached from religious (or irreligious) teaching or practice (1975: 27).

"Liberal" in liberal democracy distinguishes it from democracy that is not liberal, or "illiberal," as are most post-colonial states.[3] The political philosophy of liberalism preceded the historical evolution of liberal democratic state as modern Europe emerged from the seventeenth century onwards. Liberalism, as political philosophy in defence of individual rights and freedom, distinguishes modern politics and society from pre-modern or traditional societies and from those societies in modern times that look backwards in elevating some variation of collectivism. The ancient struggle between individual and collective assumes a radically new dimension in the modern historical

---

[3] F. Zakaria, "The Rise of Illiberal Democracy," *Foreign Affairs*, November-December 1997, pp. 22-43.

period, and though the origin of liberalism is coincident with the modern world its roots might be traced back to the concept of individualism that was first expressed in ancient Greece. "Individualism," Karl Popper noted, in ancient Greek use was as an antonym of "collectivism" and not, as Plato misused it, to signify "egoism" or "selfishness." In *The Open Society and Its Enemies* Popper pointed out, "The emancipation of the individual was indeed the great spiritual revolution which had led to the breakdown of tribalism and to the rise of democracy" (1971: 101). This individualism, contrary to Plato's opinion, was not lacking in altruism nor was it selfish, as demonstrated by Pericles of Athens whose words Popper quoted, "We are taught...never to forget that we must protect the injured" (ibid: 102). Moreover, Popper wrote:

This individualism, united with altruism, has become the basis of our western civilization. It is the central doctrine of Christianity ('love your neighbour', say the Scriptures, not 'love your tribe'); and it is the core of all ethical doctrines which have grown from our civilization and stimulated it. It is also, for instance, Kant's central practical doctrine ('always recognize that human individuals are ends, and do not use them as mere means to your ends'). There is no other thought which has been so powerful in the moral development of man (ibid).

Hence, from individualism of ancient Greece to liberalism in the age of the Protestant Reformation and the Enlightenment, the one common element in the development of modern liberal philosophy was the emancipation of the *generic* man from the collectivist hold of tribe, caste, church, nation, class and any ideology that made of him a mere cog in a wheel. It is relevant, and also important to emphasize here, the idea of "individual" and "individualism" that Popper described was not acknowledged or recognized by any of the non-Western civilizations — for instance, ancient India, China or Arab-Islamic — as the foundational principle of their ethics or politics, and only through prolonged and substantive contact with the West would this idea enter into non-Western societies.

Liberalism in modern times, and particularly in its Anglo-American variety somewhat distinct from that in continental Europe, stands for the best possible political arrangement in the relationship of individual and state in which the individual is least constrained by the state and most advantageously situated for his own advancement. The modern state is a technologically oriented state, supported and strengthened by modern science, and is by the nature and circumstances of its origin centralizing in terms of its scope and authority. It was against the background of such an emergent modern state that liberalism was formulated in its English-Scottish setting in the writings of John Locke (1632-1704), David Hume (1711-76) and Adam Smith (1723-90). Their thinking surfaced in the American Revolution of 1776 and in the making of the American republic and its constitution, while the practical aspects of liberal politics found expression in the *Federalist Papers*. Canadian politics was also similarly influenced, and despite differences in the political arrangements between Canada and the United States both countries were established on foundations supportive of liberalism emphasizing individual rights and freedom (Gairdner 2010: 27-35).

For proponents of multiculturalism the task then has been to demonstrate that expanding the concept of individual rights and freedom by including group or collective demand for recognition on the basis of respecting "diversity" or "politics of difference" does not violate liberalism as broadly understood and accepted since the eighteenth century. This task is at once political and philosophical; political as it arises from exigencies of the contemporary world and the situation in which a liberal democracy such as Canada finds itself, and philosophical since political choices if they are not to be opportunistic need to be grounded on clearly articulated principles that transcend the requirements of the moment. In meeting this demand or challenge the most interesting contributions are to be found in the writings of the Canadians Charles Taylor (1992) and Will Kymlicka (2007, 1995), the British Bhiku Parekh (2000), and the Australian Chandran Kukathas (2003). It is not possible here to explore at any length their work and, thereby, do justice to their writings which deserve careful reading. Briefly the main thrust of the argument arises from the view that liberalism is evolutionary, its ideas of rights and freedoms are not contrary to the demands of social justice, and its emphasis on securing individual liberty does not and cannot mean denial of rights and freedom to *minorities* in contemporary societies on the basis of recognizing the legitimacy of group or collective demands. The "progressive" climate in politics of the 1960s prepared the ground for the expansive revision of liberalism to accommodate changes in society that grew in time and pressured governments for reforms. According to Parekh,

The last four decades of the twentieth century witnessed the emergence of a cluster of intellectual and political movements led by such diverse groups as the indigenous peoples, national minorities, ethno-cultural nations, old and new immigrants, feminists, gay men and lesbians, and the greens. They represent practices, life-styles, views and ways of life that are different from, disapproved of, and in varying degrees discouraged by the dominant culture of the wider society. Although they are too disparate to share a common philosophical and political agenda, they are all united in resisting the wider society's homogenizing or assimilationist thrust based on the belief that there is only one correct, true or normal way to understand and structure the relevant areas of life. In their own different ways they want society to recognize the legitimacy of their differences, especially those that in their view are not incidental and trivial but spring from and constitute their identities (2000:1).

Change tends to be irresistible, and resisting changes that Parekh described on the basis of liberalism would have meant, ironically, turning the political philosophy most supportive of freedom on its head into opposing freedom. This would be contrary to the "progressive" climate of the time, and so bit by bit the argument for society open to demands viewed as legitimate meant the case for multiculturalism was self-evident and became irrefutable.

Chapter Two

THE NEW POLITICS OF IDENTITY

Liberalism at the beginning meant, as Robert Heilbroner writing about Adam Smith in his popular study of "worldly philosophers" noted, an ideology supporting "a system of perfect liberty" (1999: 42). While such a system might have been an ideal imagined by Adam Smith and others influenced by his work, there was a time in modern history when this ideal was as nearly realized as in England in the period before 1914. It is worthwhile recalling that period, since from the perspective of the early years of the twenty-first century the memory of that history has faded away with the result that anyone politically making the case for securing liberalism as the system most advantageous for the freedom of individual would seem utopian, if not reactionary, to a great many people today. Of this period remarkable for its liberal or "individualist" characteristics historian A.J.P. Taylor wrote:

Until August 1914 a sensible, law-abiding Englishman could pass through life and hardly notice the existence of the state, beyond the post office and the policeman. He could live where he liked and as he liked. He had no official number or identity card. He could travel abroad or leave his country forever without a passport or any sort of official permission. He could exchange his money for any other currency without restriction or limit. He could buy goods from any country in the world on the same terms as he bought goods at home. For that matter, a foreigner could spend his life in this country without permit and without informing the police. Unlike the countries of the European continent, the state did not require its citizens to perform military service. An Englishman could enlist, if he chose, in the regular army, the navy, or the territorials. He could also ignore, if he chose, the demands of national defence. Substantial householders were occasionally called on for jury service. Otherwise, only those helped the state who wished to do so...broadly speaking, the state acted only to help those who could not help themselves. It left the adult citizen alone (1965: 1).

The England Taylor described was lost in the immense upheavals of the twentieth century which another historian, Eric Hobsbawm, labeled as the "age of extremes" (1995). Under the impact of two world wars, the great depression, the rise of totalitarian political systems (Nazism and Communism) and the making of welfare states, liberalism was forced to give ground to collectivist arguments in the making of an increasingly interventionist state. The England of Taylor's description was the closest approximation of a modern industrial democracy being minimalist or the "night-watchman" state. In such a minimalist state individuals would find, as Isaiah Berlin wrote, the "wider the area of non-interference the wider my freedom" (1969: 123). And while England of the late nineteenth and early twentieth century represented the high noon of liberalism, it nevertheless stood for the privilege of the "white men" despite the reforms of the Victorian era. It would take another generation before liberalism became inclusive of women by extending to the female half of the population the right to vote. In the United Kingdom women's right to vote was granted after the war in 1918, and only after 1928 the parliament gave women full equal right as men to vote. In the United States the nineteenth amendment ratified in 1920 extended to women the full equal right to vote, and Canada would do the same in 1921 (Flexner, 1975; Lloyd, 1971). The struggle for women to acquire voting rights in liberal democracies showed liberalism is a work in progress, never quite complete as the concept of freedom and equal rights are claimed by those individuals and groups excluded from representation.

Yet Taylor's England illustrated the core liberal principle of individual freedom in society protected by the rule of law. At its simplest this idea of individual freedom as the worthiest goal of politics received the most insightful and lucid treatment in the writings of F.A. Hayek, the Austrian economist, philosopher and co-winner of the Nobel Memorial Prize in Economics in 1974. In defining freedom, Hayek wrote in his majestic work, *The Constitution of Liberty,*

It so happens that the meaning of freedom that we have adopted seems to be the original meaning of the word. Man, or at least European man, enters history divided into free and unfree; and this distinction had a very definite meaning. The freedom of the free may have differed widely, but only in the degree of an independence which the slave did not possess at all. It meant always the possibility of a person's acting according to his own decisions and plans, in contrast to the position of one who was irrevocably subject to the will of another, who by arbitrary decision could coerce him to act or not to act in specific ways. The time-honored phrase by which this freedom has often been described is therefore "independence of the arbitrary will of another" (2006: 12).

In Hayek's usage, as in Karl Popper's, the term "individual" refers anthropologically to the generic man, or man in essence defined by the commonly shared humanity of the species and free individual is man unbounded by any limiting condition arbitrarily imposed on him by others. Such "individual" might be historic fiction, but it is a useful premise in conceiving the sort of society that is ideally liberal and worthy of defending or constructing. As I have already noted, the reference to the generic man in the writings of liberal thinkers is uncluttered by any attribute of specificity in terms of ethnicity, religion, gender, sexual orientation or any other "identity" marker that comes into vogue in the second-half of the twentieth century. The claim on behalf of the generic man is universal, the concept of freedom as Hayek provides is universal and, therefore, the appeal of liberal democracy is universal.

The supporters of liberalism were exercised by any abridgement of individual freedom brought about by demands of the state or society. In this sense the conception of liberty distinctively understood as freedom by classical liberal thinkers, writes John Gray in *Liberalism*, "is wholly or predominantly a negative one" (1995: 56). The conception of "negative" liberty as distinct from "positive" liberty rests on the difference "between noninterference and independence on the one hand and an entitlement to participate in collective decision-making on the other hand" (ibid). This initial difference might be small enough to be negligible in terms of consequences for the eventual meaning of liberalism, yet the constructionist imperative — the provision of resources by the state or its interventions required to remove any, or all, impediments in society on the basis of engendering *equality* — to assist individuals in their self-realization that is embedded in the politics of "positive" liberty, paradoxically, tends toward expanding the interventionist power of the state over individuals. The tension between the two concepts of liberty once it was identified, or once it was understood the idea of freedom *from interference* is distinct and not to be confused with the idea of freedom *to do* or *acquire* something, has remained with us. Berlin discussed this tension in his widely read essay "Two Concepts of Liberty," and in it he explored the appeal of "positive" over "negative" liberty. He contended that any sacrifice of individual freedom made for any other worthy cause be it equality, justice or the amelioration of any form of misery such as disease and poverty, does not bring an increase in freedom since "a sacrifice is not an increase in what is being sacrificed, namely freedom, however great the moral need or the compensation for it. Everything is what it is: liberty is liberty, not equality or fairness or justice or culture, or human happiness or a quiet conscience" (Berlin: 125).

The expansion of freedom to all people, in other words assisting people denied freedom on whatever basis to be free as individuals and live free uncoerced arbitrarily by anyone or any institution save by the naturally endowed capacity in human beings for reasoning and the instinct for self-preservation, remains the core irreducible principle of liberalism. On this basis both England of Taylor's description and the United States of Abraham Lincoln were liberal societies, yet flawed and deficient to the extent of freedom denied to a large portion of the people. Denying women the right to vote and keeping "Negroes" as slaves were politically illiberal and ethically indefensible. Their emancipation, however delayed, when it came was consistent with liberal philosophy even though, in both instances, the struggle to gain freedom meant negating restrictions imposed on women and slaves on the basis of "identity" markers of gender and colour respectively. But viewed in terms of Berlin's opinion on liberty, freedom for women and slaves did not entail any sacrifice or diminution of freedom in general, and in extending freedom to women and slaves justice was done that repaired the flaw, as a result of historical circumstances, in liberalism. In both the cases of women acquiring the right to vote and slaves emancipated from bondage liberalism displayed its capacity for self-correction regardless of the cost, and in the process the gap between the reality and the ideal of liberalism was reduced. This capacity of self-correction illustrates the open-ended nature of liberalism to bring about the inclusion into liberal society of excluded groups as free individuals, such as women and slaves who were once denied freedom. It might be said of nineteenth century England and the United States that as advanced models of liberal democracy they showed to the rest of the world the hopeful image of the future in terms of liberalism and its promise of freedom for individuals. Indeed this promise as the liberal creed was felt most keenly for the longest time by Jews and, despite their difficulties too many to describe here, they viewed that a liberal society such as England and the United States offered them most security as a free people. This view might be highly contentious among Jews in the post-Holocaust history and with the establishment of Israel, yet such a view has much resonance with nearly half of the total number of Jews worldwide who reside in the United States. Indeed Jacob Neusner, one of the most prolific scholars of Judaism and Jewish history and a noncongregational rabbi, argued in his book *Who, Where and What is "Israel"?* that "to be a Jew and to be truly free means to live in the United States of America or in other nations that meet its high standard of freedom" (1989: ix).

II.

The opposition to liberalism has come from those who hold on to collectivist doctrines, most compelling of which are those of nationalism and socialism. In both instances the collective interests of the *nation* and *class* are juxtaposed against the right of individual to be free.

For socialists liberalism represents the narrow class interest of the *bourgeoisie* — the merchants of capital and owners or shareholders of private property — and, therefore, liberal ideology functions on behalf of those who benefit most from, as the Canadian political theorist C.B. Macpherson described it, "possessive individualism." While socialists concede liberalism is an historical advance over ideologies representing pre-capitalist systems, they contend following Marx liberalism itself needs to be transcended by socialism in making the working class as the largest segment of population in society *substantively* free — not merely free in the *formal* and narrowly legal sense in a liberal society — by collectivizing the ownership of capital with the means of state control. The emergence of the working class movement armed with the socialist ideology posed the most immediately serious challenge to liberalism from the last quarter of the nineteenth century to the eventual collapse of the socialist experiment under communists with the disintegration of the former Union of Soviet Socialist Republics (the Soviet Union) in the final decade of the twentieth century.

Nationalism, however, has remained the more insidious challenge to liberalism since its claim is not a frontal assault on liberal state and society as is the socialist challenge. The claim of nationalism is political, as Gellner pointed out, with nationalists insisting "the political and national unit should be congruent" (1983: 1). Consequently, nationalism can wear the garment of liberal ideology as readily or convincingly as it may be dressed up in any "illiberal" or anti-liberal collectivist ideology. The insidiousness of nationalism as an ideology springs from its essential nature of being a sentimental expression of a people asserting group identity that is at once modern and primordial. Moreover, and decidedly, nationalism is the first compellingly important mobilizing ideology in modern history based on *identity* politics. Nationalist sentiment accompanies the rise and consolidation of the modern state in transition from an agrarian to an industrial society, and in this complex relationship of *nation* and *state* the question which comes first is a conundrum. Both have been contingent on one another as one theorist of identity politics explained, since the "state sought the obedience of its subjects by representing itself as the fulfillment of the nation's destiny and a guarantee of its continuation. On the other hand, a nation without a state would be bound to be unsure of its past, insecure in its present and uncertain of its future, and so doomed to a precarious existence" (Bauman: 21).

The ancient love of one's native land was tied to the natural attachment with the world into which one was born. The absence in anyone of this primordial affection to one's birthplace would be noticed as unnatural, just as the appearance of a stranger in a world where people's mobility was limited to the immediate surroundings of their rural home would be noticed as curious. This affection, attachment or sense of belonging marked an individual for his life as member of a clan or a tribe, and set him apart from other similar groups. And when enlarged to embrace others beyond one's tribe, it became the love of a patriot for his country. Sir Walter Scott (1771-1832) — the much loved Scottish poet-novelist writing during the period when England and Scotland together were at the head of the great transition from agrarian to industrial age that set Europe apart from the rest of the world — captured poignantly the natural feelings for this ancient love of one's birthplace, and the unnaturalness when it is absent in any individual, in the opening verse of the sixth canto of his long narrative poem "The Lay of the Last Minstrel":

Breathes there the man, with soul so dead,
Who never to himself hath said,
This is my own, my native land!
Whose heart hath ne'er within him burn'd,
As home his footsteps he hath turn'd,
From wandering on a foreign strand!
If such there breathe, go, mark him well;
For him no Minstrel raptures swell;
High though his titles, proud his name,
Boundless his wealth as wish can claim;
Despite those titles, power, and pelf,
The wretch, concentrated all in self,
Living, shall forfeit fair renown,
And, doubly dying, shall go down
To the vile dust, from whence he sprung,
Unwept, unhonour'd, and unsung.

From Scott's poetic rendition of the ancient love for native land to the German philosopher Johann Gottlieb Fichte's (1762-1814) "Addresses to the German Nation" there is a leap of imagination, philosophical and political, that turns the simple sense of attachment to a particular patch of earth into an ethnic identity out of which is born modern nationalism. Nationalism may not be entirely the product of imagining past history in terms of ethnicity, yet imagination plays a large role in the making of nationalist sentiment and launching political movements on its behalf for statehood.

The origin and growth of nationalism is too broad and varied to be explained within a single theory, yet there is a shared understanding among recent writers on the subject of how nationalism has proven to be so potent due to the appeal of an imagined past in the drawing and re-drawing of the political map of our world (Anderson, 1991; Smith, 1991). Ethnicity or ethnic identity has also proven to be far more potent in politically mobilizing people than class identity. This potency arises from the emotional pull of ethnic identity as an internal disposition in human beings acting as agents of history in shaping their world, whereas class identity as an objectively provided sociological category of socialist politics is lacking the emotionalism of nationalist politics.

Nationalist identity also serves well the modern state as it is assimilative even when it is not culturally homogenizing. The past in nationalist politics and historiography dissolves into myth, becomes fiction, and emerges as political doctrine because the manufactured identity of the past is ever so plastic to meet whatever purposes nationalism as an ideology derives from the past for the present and the future (Bauman: 20). Take the case of India — a continent of a country in size, population, ethnic and racial diversity, plurality of languages, mix of religions, and variety of traditions and cultures — as an example of nationalist enterprise. In the writings, for instance, of Jawaharlal Nehru, India's first prime minister, the country is presented despite its long and multifaceted history as one possessing an irreducible, timeless and enduring identity provided and shaped by "Bharat Mata" (Mother India). Nehru's *The Discovery of India* is an example of nationalist imagination at work packing into one volume several thousand years of history and people as diverse as dark-skinned Dravidians and Afghan-Turkic-Mughal warriors as Indians, while their particular history is rendered as so many tributaries flowing and merging into one grand narrative as if pre-ordained into the making of modern India. The imagining of a separate Muslim state, Pakistan, by Muslim nationalists, and their demand that led to the partitioning of British India on the basis of Muhammad Ali Jinnah's "two-nation" theory, was similarly a nationalist enterprise in opposition to the imaginings of Nehru and his party, the Indian National Congress.

The example of India further illustrates how an imagined identity, that of being *Indian*, as an instrument of nationalist politics gets imposed on the entire population living within the boundaries of the modern independent state of India. But the Indian example is not unique in terms of nationalist politics since national identity was similarly put into effect in the making of the modern nation-states of

Europe. India, however, is part of that collection of post-colonial countries which Clifford Geertz labeled as "old societies and new states" (1963); these are countries in transition from agrarian-based economy to industrial economy in the years since the end of the Second World War and the beginning of de-colonization. In holding together a vastly diverse and multicultural country through the complex historical process of this transition, the nationalist ideology at work in India has played the role of a modernizing instrument assimilating or integrating the people into a state provided identity. Hence, it seems to me following Gellner and in keeping the example of India in perspective, nationalism as an ideology, first in Europe and then outside of Europe, was a positively critical input in the transitional process required for old societies to successfully emerge as modernizing new states. Yet in this hugely consequential relationship between modernization of traditional societies and the role of nationalism, it was the former that received most attention by the founders of sociology — August Comte (1798-1857), Karl Marx (1818-83), Herbert Spencer (1820-1903), Ferdinand Toennies (1855-1936), Georg Simmel (1858-1918), and Max Weber (1864-1920). This is not altogether surprising since state or nation building with nationalism and national identity as its corollary were taken together by the founders of sociology to be the objective reality of modernization as a global historical phenomenon that required theoretical explanation. The issue of identity emerging as a problem or challenge independent of the modernization process is a recent development found in generally more advanced modern (or post-modern) societies of Europe and North America, and not in India where the unfinished work of building a modern society poses major problems that early modernizers once dealt with.

III.

The question about identity of things and persons is as old and confounding as when Heraclitus, the ancient Greek philosopher from sixth century B.C., reputedly pondered on the nature of permanence and change. The idea that all of matter is in a state of flux is attributed to Heraclitus's observation that an individual could not step into the same river twice with water in constant flow, and since then philosophers have discussed the problem of identity in terms of "how anything could persist through change" (Brody: 3). If no one thing remains the same, if all things and persons are given to change, hence there is no such thing existing as immutable and ever-lasting (save God, or the idea of God), then how are we to know and recognize things or persons at different instants of time? Plato posed this problem as an eternal paradox in *Timaeus* stating the need to distinguish "between that which always is and never becomes from that which is always becoming but never is" (1965: 40). Yet in asking what is that which never becomes by defying change, or remains resistant to change, takes us into the realm of metaphysics and speculative theology; the answer, therefore, to the question "Who am I" or "Know thyself", as Socrates instructed, remains elusive.

The question of identity nevertheless persists despite philosophical difficulties and epistemological problems, and at the common sense level people are more or less satisfied with the answer that things and persons are known by their properties. For humans, their properties are not only physiological as provided by nature but also mental acquired through learning and teaching. Hence, the question "Who am I" raises all the related matter of what I have been *taught* as a child since birth by parents, relatives, teachers, and society outside of the family that provides for my sense of belonging or attachment to familiar surroundings, and what I have *learned* of my self and my relationship with others in this world where I make my home. The epistemological and philosophical problems relating to identity do not dissolve by relying on common sense, but it is a beginning hopefully based on some reliable facts as given or acquired. It is in the passage or development from being simply human by the fact of what nature biologically has provided us with, to becoming human by the process of education and learning acquired that we make of ourselves who we are.

The most important attribute of being human is provided by the faculty of mind to acquire language, and this presupposes the capacity of the mind to store and recall information or, in other words, *memory*; and, in addition to improvising and learning language, it is inventiveness in *tool-making* that sets humans on the path of making the world of their choice with the raw material provided by nature. Memory, according to some, is the important constitutive element in the question of identity (Shoemaker: chapters 4 and 5; Miri: 1-20). But memory in human terms is not merely an organic response to body or mental stimuli, or a mere recognition of the external world or recall of experience that animals also possess.

"Memory implies," Cassirer wrote, "a process of recognition and identification, an ideational process of a very complex sort" (1944: 50). This capacity in man by the ingenuity of his memory to recall and re-live past is a creative process that allows him to mould and re-mould his identity. Again Cassirer:

In man we cannot describe recollection as a simple return of an event, as a faint image or copy of former impressions. It is not simply a repetition but rather a rebirth of the past; it implies a creative and constructive process. It is not enough to pick up isolated data of our past experience; we must really *re-collect* them, we must organize and synthesize them, and assemble them into a focus of thought. It is this kind of recollection which gives us the characteristic human shape of memory, and distinguishes it from all the other phenomena in animal or organic life (ibid: 51; italics given).

But there are problems associated with the subject of memory as constitutive element of personal or group identity. There are questions surrounding the mechanics of memory, of who the person doing the recalling is and what is known of him, of how weak or strong is the recollection of the past, the veracity of such recollection, the contextualization of the past recalled and reconstructed, the task of interpreting what is remembered, the selective aspect of recollecting the past history or experiences and to what purpose. It is not my intent here to discuss any of the various aspects of the "memory" problem, while also putting aside the sort of problem arising when a person or group suffers *loss* of memory for a variety of reasons such as neurological defect in individuals or selective propaganda and air-brushing of history by those in power, except to underscore the relatedness of memory to identity

The past is instructive about who I am or, as the philosopher Alasdair MacIntyre stated, "I am born with a past" (1981: 205). But recollecting the past through the mechanics of memory is not trouble free. Indeed, as with Sophocles' greatest tragedy, *Oedipus the King*, recollecting the past can be excruciatingly painful and disjointing for the identity of the person involved. Anthony Smith takes the story of

Oedipus as the point of entry into his study of "national identity" indicating the play's central theme is about identity. He writes:

There are many motifs, and more than one level, in Sophocles' play. But the question of identity, collective as well as individual, broods over the action. 'I will know who I am': the discovery of self is the play's motor and the action's inner meaning. But each 'self' that Oedipus uncovers is also a social self, a category and a role, even when it proves to be erroneous for Oedipus. Only after the shattering revelation of 'who he is' does he begin to glimpse the meaning of his destiny (1991: 3).

Smith's recourse to Sophocles' *Oedipus* in analyzing identity is instructive and illuminating. Identity, as in Oedipus's case, is contingent on memory of events recalled and their meanings discovered, and in the process the identity of Oedipus is illuminated as not fixed but malleable. From the confined space of an amphitheatre where myths and imagined tales are enacted to the real world of people at work and play, being alive means giving expression to one's discovered or constructed identity as an individual or as member of a group. But to the extent real life mimics the theatre instead of the other way around, the thrill in the confidence of knowing one's identity in terms of origin, or belonging, or abilities, or belief is accompanied by the fear or anxiety of its loss brought about by changing circumstances wrought by time or by disclosures from the past that is tragically revelatory as in Sophocles' play about Oedipus, the King of Thebes.

Hence, the old persistent question, "Who am I", might be re-phrased as to "What is my identity" beyond that which is biologically determined. In discovering one's identity an individual engages with his past through memory, and this engagement is not a solitary labour, a monologue in solitary space; it is instead a dialogue with other individuals living at present and those once living through the artifice of memory. The search for knowledge of self leads to philosophy, and discovery of one's identity becomes in part a dialogical process of interaction with others as in the case of Oedipus making his self-discovery in despair. In the case of Macbeth, as another example from literature, his identities are announced in the encounter with the witches, and then he sets out to claim them by his choice of deeds. In the real world identity as a predicate provided by others might be insufficient or constraining of what one prefers as a result of knowledge acquired, and thus effort is directed through work by extending oneself in the making of one's identity.

The salient fact about memory in the making of individual identity, and to lesser extent group identity, is how much of identity in a world of flux is fluid. Memory may not only play tricks or be deceptive and unreliable, memory is selective, celebratory, traumatic, self-serving, comforting, and factual, and out of this woven fabric of recollections an individual stitches the garment of his identity which he wears for the world to take notice of and acknowledge him for who he is. Here is Amin Maalouf, a highly regarded novelist and winner in 1993 of the prestigious French literary honour, Prix Goncourt, describing his identity. Maalouf writes:

I sometimes find myself "examining my identity" as other people examine their conscience. As you may imagine, my object is not to discover within myself some "essential" allegiance in which I may recognize myself. Rather the opposite; I scour my memory to find as many ingredients of my identity as I can. I then assemble and arrange them. I don't deny any of them.

I come from a family which originated in the southern part of the Arab world and which for centuries lived in the mountains of Lebanon. More recently, by a series of migrations, it has spread out to various other parts of the world, from Egypt to Brazil and from Cuba to Australia. It takes pride in having always been at once Arab and Christian, and this probably since the second or third century A.D. — that is, long before the rise of Islam and even before the West was converted to Christianity.

The fact of simultaneously being Christian and having as my mother tongue Arabic, the holy language of Islam, is one of the basic paradoxes that have shaped my own identity. Speaking Arabic creates bonds between me and all those who use it every day in their prayers, though most of them by far don't know it as well as I do...

This language is common to us all — to him, to me and to more than a billion others. On the other hand, my being a Christian — regardless of whether I am so out of deep religious conviction or merely for sociological reasons — also creates a significant link between me and the two billion or so other Christians in the world. There are many things in which I differ from every Christian, every Arab and every Muslim, but between me and each of them there is also an undeniable kinship, in one case religious and intellectual and in the other linguistic and cultural.

That said, the fact of being at once an Arab and a Christian puts one in a very special situation: it makes you a member of a minority — a situation not always easy to accept. It marks a person deeply and permanently...

Thus, when I think about either of these two components of my identity separately, I feel close either through language or through religion to a good half of the human race. But when I take the same two elements together, I find myself face to face with my own specificity.

I could say the same thing about other ties. I share the fact that I'm French with 60 million or so others; the fact that I'm Lebanese with between eight and ten million, if you include the diaspora; but with how many do I share the fact that I'm both French and Lebanese? With a few thousand, at most (2001: 16-18).

Maalouf's recollections of his past make of his identity a composite picture of someone at once unique in some ways yet linked to people through a shared language and culture. This composite identity of a *hybrid*-individual is increasingly the effect of a highly mobile world that makes for a modern egalitarian society (Gellner: 24-25). Salman Rushdie, the Indian-born British writer and winner of the prestigious English literary prize, the 1981 Booker Prize, received a death sentence pronounced by Ayatollah Khomeini, the Iranian religious leader, for his novel *The Satanic Verses* allegedly transgressing the boundary of what is sacred in Islam. This novel about the imagined identities of its protagonists was read as insulting to Islam and its prophet by a vast number of Muslims, and Rushdie was forced into hiding in fear for his life. About his novel Rushdie wrote:

Standing at the center of the novel is a group of characters most of whom are British Muslims, or not particularly religious persons of Muslim background, struggling with just the sort of great problems that have arisen to surround the book, problems of hybridization and ghettoization, of reconciling the old and the new. Those who oppose the novel most vociferously today are of the opinion that intermingling with a different culture will inevitably weaken and ruin their own. I am of the opposite opinion. *The Satanic Verses* celebrates hybridity, impurity, intermingling, the transformation that comes of new and unexpected combinations of human beings, cultures, ideas, politics, movies, songs. It rejoices in mongrelization and fears the absolutism of the Pure. *Melange*, hotpotch, a bit of this and a bit of that is *how newness enters the world*. It is the great possibility that mass migration gives the world, and I have tried to embrace it. *The Satanic Verses* is for change-by-fusion, change-by-conjoining. It is a love-song to our mongrel selves (1992: 394; italics given).

The matter of identity of individuals in the modern world of mobility and choice, following Maalouf and Rushdie, is increasingly pluralistic, fluid and can well be volatile. Since identity is greatly contingent on memory it is an act of imagination, and how lurid, or powerful, or evocative, the act is will vary from individual to individual and from circumstance to circumstance.

IV.

The need to know "Who am I" is one-half of the equation in the process of discovering and asserting my identity, the other-half rests with the need that others recognize me for who I am. The need for recognition, Charles Taylor has argued, is important, as is memory, in the formation of identity of individuals and groups. He observed, "our identity is partly shaped by recognition or its absence, often by misrecognition of others, and so a person or group of people can suffer real damage, real distortion, if the people or society around them mirror back to them a confusing or demeaning or contemptible picture of themselves" (1992: 25). Recognition of oneself by another at the minimum duly confirms one's specifically imagined or constructed existence, and makes an opening for dialogue. Simple recognition brings with it confirmation of who I am, to which group I belong in terms of my ethnicity, nationality or any other externally provided marker of my identity, and that as an individual I am capable of acting out of my own volition.

But the politics of recognition, in Charles Taylor's view, is weightier than mere acknowledgement of the other. One of the characteristics of the modern world is the leveling of hierarchies in society that marked out social relationships in the pre-modern or traditional world of social inequalities. Hierarchies indicated the privileges of an *honour*-bound society, and in such society recognition of an individual meant relatively less of who he is than his place as part of a group in the hierarchical standing of estate, class or caste in society. The modern world conversely, according to Charles Taylor, is one where *dignity* is the democratic value to be shared equally by all in society. Consequently, the felt need or demand of individuals and groups for recognition is about being received by others, especially those in power, with dignity as equal in society and in law (1992: 27). Recognition therefore as an element of politics in liberal-democracy legitimates individual or group identity, and in the process removes those barriers that excluded them from being full and equal members of society.

Affirming the dignity of the other as equal means accepting the other for what he is or wants to be individually or as member of a group, in other words accepting what makes him or the group he belongs to *different* from the rest. Hence politics of recognition is also in effect politics dealing with differences within society alongside the tension that accompanies such politics. And since such politics in the modern world is driven by the democratic impulse affirming equality of individuals, the politics of recognition makes identity politics predominantly into a phenomenon of liberal democracy.

Here it is worth noting nationalism and its demands for recognition have been the dominant form of identity politics in the making of the modern world of nation-states or state-nations. It can be said that nationalism is the most potent expression of identity politics. And whenever or wherever a people, as in Quebec within Canada, espouse nationalism there exist politics of separatism and division. There is of course irony in such politics. It is rare — practically never, though the world has witnessed the exceptional case of the peaceful dissolution of the former state of Czechoslovakia in 1992 into the republics of Czech and Slovakia — that once nationalists are recognized and their demand for self-determination fulfilled they are agreeable to peacefully concede the same to another group on the basis of identity politics. Such is the irony, for instance, when Quebec nationalist-separatists with their demand to disengage from Canada on the grounds of Quebecois nationalism are unwilling to acknowledge that the Cree and Inuit Indians of northern Quebec would have their rights on the same grounds to separate from Quebec in forming a state of their own or remaining within Canada.

Identity politics is also about freedom, of expanding the boundaries of freedom in society for an individual to be recognized for who he is or who he wants to be, and for including groups denied freedom. As I noted, the United States as an example of liberal democracy has demonstrated the capacity for self-correction when it abolished slavery and granted women equal rights as men to vote. Hence, theoretically speaking, no liberal democracy will impede, or persist in impeding, extending recognition to individuals affirming their dignity as full and equal members of society. Any impediment within a liberal democracy denying the equal worth and dignity of individuals can only be the persistence of anti-democratic prejudices that once exposed to public scrutiny should crumble. Indeed it is liberalism, and wherever it has been introduced, that has proven to be the most effective solvent of impediments denying the worth of individuals as free human beings in theory, if not entirely in the practical world of politics. The flaws of liberal democracy, in this sense, are merely the reflection of human imperfection.

The demand for recognition that Isaiah Berlin observed as the "search for status" in modern politics, however, cannot be confined to individuals. The sentiment driving the demand of an individual for recognition is his quest to be free, while in the non-recognition or mis-recognition of his identity he feels confined and not free. But he also feels and thinks his freedom is denied or is insufficient if the group to which he belongs is also denied recognition and freedom. Here what is involved is the existential reality of an individual who sees the completeness of his identity is bound with that of the group identity he is attached to by kinship relations or ideology, and any non-recognition or mis-recognition of the group identity is also a diminution of his identity as a free human being. About this Berlin wrote:

I may feel unfree in the sense of not being recognized as a self-governing individual human being; but I may feel it also as a member of an unrecognized or insufficiently respected group: then I wish for the emancipation of my entire class, or community, or nation, or race, or profession. So much can I desire this, that I may, in my bitter longing for status, prefer to be bullied and misgoverned by some member of my own race or social class, by whom I am, nevertheless, recognized as a man and a rival — that is as an equal — to being well and tolerantly treated by someone from some higher and remoter group, who does not recognize me for what I wish to feel myself to be. This is the heart of the great cry for recognition on the part of both individuals and groups, and in our own day, of professions and classes, nations and races... It is this desire for reciprocal recognition that leads the most authoritarian democracies to be, at times, consciously preferred by its members to the most enlightened oligarchies, or sometime causes a member of some newly liberated Asian or African state to complain less today, when he is rudely treated by members of his own race or nation, than when he was governed by some cautious, just, gentle, well-meaning administrator from outside. Unless this phenomenon is grasped, the ideals and behaviour of entire peoples who, in Mill's sense of the word, suffer deprivation of elementary human rights, and who, with every appearance of sincerity, speak of enjoying more freedom than when they possessed a wider measure of these rights, becomes an unintelligible paradox (1969: 157-158).

It is this liberal sensibility at work when recognition is extended to individuals that the same is also extended to groups, or when in expanding the boundary of freedom for individuals the same argument for group freedom is also made. It was this sensibility at work that contributed in large measure, if not entirely, to the relatively swift end of European empires in Asia and Africa and the success of nationalist movements there. This is because the liberal argument for recognition and freedom, as Martin Luther King, Jr. understood well, is not divisible or selective.

In the second half of the twentieth century a consensus was reached among a segment of liberal thinkers that the meaning of liberalism required broadening of the struggle for freedom to emancipate individuals from the grip of authoritarian control of collectivist politics that went all the way back to ancient Greece, to including the struggle for social justice. Simply put most liberal thinkers agreed with Kant, and contrary to Aristotle, that an individual is an end for himself and not means for the end of someone else; in other words, the rights and freedom of individual take precedence over that of society and state. But, as Berlin showed, there is a difference in the conceiving of freedom as "negative" liberty or as "positive" liberty. The broadening of the notion of liberalism to include demand for the collective recognition of group rights meant a shift in emphasis in favour of "positive" liberty. It is this broadening of the notion of liberalism that prepared the grounds for identity politics to become the instrument for pushing a liberal society, such as Canada, to accept the argument in terms of public policy for multiculturalism, to concede that the politics of recognition must be extended to groups and not be limited to individuals only.

V.

A good society is also deemed to be a just society. What is meant by good society has been a matter of much discussion in the making of the modern world or, more precisely, in the transition of Europe from the pre-modern to the modern world. How "good" was understood in the pre-modern world before the age of European enlightenment was substantively different than how "good" has come to be defined in modern times. The difference lies in the two differing mentalities, one pre-modern and the other modern. This fact is important, since the meaning of justice based on the concept of good society differs in respect to the two mentalities.

One of the defining characteristics of the pre-modern world was the place of religion in the manner in which society was ordered. Religion anchored man to his place in the world and the hereafter, brought him comfort in the knowledge of good and evil derived from his faith in a supernatural Being, provided him explanation of the physical world around him based on the metaphysics of his belief system, and linked him in the "great chain of being" that flows outward from the plenitude of the supernatural Being in an hierarchy of creation from angels through human beings to the simplest or lowliest form of life (Lovejoy: chapter III). It was the *order* provided by religious knowledge that was *good*, and that which pertained to *goodness* in such an ordered society was *just*. Justice then was doing good or what contributed to the well-being of order implicit in the idea of the "great chain of being," in preventing evil, and in penalizing anyone who did or contributed to doing what was deemed evil on the basis of instructions provided by the religious system to which an individual belonged.

The pre-modern world was, as Max Weber described, an enchanted place and the ultimate knowledge resided with the learning and knowing of what constituted the highest good. In this effort Plato's philosophy was considered indispensable. According to Arthur

Lovejoy, "there is no question as to the nature of Plato's historic influence; the completely 'other' and 'ineffable' One,' the Absolute of the Neo-platonists, it is certain, was for those philosophers, and their many later echoers, medieval and modern, Jewish, Moslem, and Christian, an interpretation of Plato's 'Idea of the Good'" (1964: 39-40). And the "Idea of the Good" in the "Form of the Good is the universal object of desire, that which draws all souls towards itself; and that the chief good for man even in this life is nothing but the contemplation of this absolute or essential Good" (ibid: 41). The meaning of good was ultimately an attribute of God, as was the meaning of justice.

The making of the modern world is a break with the idea of the "great chain of being" and all that it implied. The experimental method of modern science displaces religious knowledge, and this leads to the arrangement of politics and society on the basis of the new philosophy that sets Europe apart in the age of Enlightenment from its earlier history. Weber introduced the term *rationalization* to describe the process in the shift from the pre-modern to the modern world, and *rationality* as one of its chief defining characteristics (Gerth and Mills: 51-55). The historic effect of this process is the separation of religion from politics with the world increasingly becoming a *dis*-enchanted place.

If the highest virtue in the pre-modern world was in contemplating the nature of good, or God, as the essential axiomatic truth from which all other propositions in philosophy, ethics and politics were derived, the analogue of this in the modern world would be contemplating the idea of freedom as the highest political good that makes it possible for man to realize for himself his full potential. The idea of freedom as man's natural right bestowed by nature or God emerges as the fundamental premise of the good society in the writings of liberal philosophers from John Locke to John Stuart Mill. A good society, in the liberal perspective, was born as a result of the social contract made by naturally born free men to exit from the state of nature which in Locke's view was unstable and prone to dissolve into a *state of war*, and thereby secure for man his natural or unalienable rights endowed by his Creator and among these were listed in America's Declaration of Independence "life, liberty and the pursuit of happiness". In other words, a society is only good insofar as it secures freedom for individuals to thrive unfettered from any arbitrary coercion or interference of another individual or of the society itself. The modern reasoning inverts the "great chain of being" and asserts man is the moral centre of his universe, and any deprivation of his rights by others is diminishing him from being the arbiter of his own destiny. The only exception, as Mill wrote, "is to prevent harm to others... The only part of the conduct of anyone for which he is amenable to society is that which concerns others. In the part which merely concerns himself, his independence is, of right, absolute. Over himself, over his own body and mind, the individual is sovereign" (1974: 68-69).

Justice then in a society ordered on the basis of the liberal principle of freedom serves the interests of free individuals. From this perspective, according to John Rawls, "Each person possesses an inviolability founded on justice that even the welfare of society as a whole cannot override. For this reason justice denies that the loss of freedom for some is made right by a greater good shared by others. It does not allow that the sacrifices imposed on a few are outweighed by the larger sum of advantages enjoyed by many. Therefore in a just society the liberties of equal citizenship are taken as settled; the rights secured by justice are not subject to political bargaining or to the calculus of social interests" (1971: 3-4).

John Rawls published his seminal work, *A Theory of Justice*, in 1971 — the year Prime Minister Trudeau's government adopted multiculturalism as Canada's official policy — and its publication gave new impetus to contemporary liberal thinking on the most fundamental question pertaining to moral philosophy. Rawls claimed "Justice is the first virtue of social institutions," and set forth the main argument in his weighty study for viewing "justice as fairness." The compelling nature of Rawls argument opened a breach between his view of what makes for the legitimacy of the liberal state and society, and the earlier views of liberal thinkers, most notably Mill, based on the premise of social contract. This pre-*Rawlsian* thinking was based on the contractarian device in establishing the legitimacy of the liberal order, and it was ultimately utilitarian as Mill conceded:

To have a right, then, is, I conceive, to have something which society ought to defend me in the possession of. If the objector goes on to ask why it ought, I can give him no other reason than general utility (1991: 189).

Though Rawls also relied on the contractarian device, his theoretical innovation was that the initial agreement reached by the contracting parties as free individuals was something more basic than the constitution of state or form of government that would be one disposed to liberal values. Rawls wrote:

My aim is to present a conception of justice which generalizes and carries to a higher level of abstraction the familiar theory of the social contract as found, say, in Locke, Rousseau, and Kant. In order to do this we are not to think of the original contract as one to enter a particular society or to set up a particular form of government. Rather, the guiding idea is that the principles of justice for the basic structure of society are the object of the original agreement. They are the principles that free and rational persons concerned to further their own interests would accept in an initial position of equality as defining the fundamental terms of their association. These principles are to regulate all further agreements; they specify the kinds of social cooperation that can be entered into and the forms of government that can be established. This way of regarding the principles of justice I shall call justice as fairness (1971: 11).

Thus the concept of justice as fairness shifted the ground for liberal thinking on the nature of the good society from the utilitarian argument of Mill based on the premise that "pleasure" or "satisfaction" of the individual is the ultimate measure of value to be promoted and secured, or the earlier argument of Locke based on the premise that God made human beings independent and equal, to the "fairness" principle that is based on moral consideration of right and wrong. Rawls explained, "We are not to gain from the cooperative labors of others without doing our fair share" and "the requirements specified by the principle of fairness are the obligations" (ibid: 112).

The importance of Rawls's contribution has been widely acclaimed. The philosopher Robert Nozick greeted Rawls's work with the observation "Political philosophers now must either work within Rawls's theory or explain why not" (1974: 183). The breach that Rawls opened allowed for the argument that "economic and social goods other than basic liberty are to be distributed so that inequalities are to the advantage of the least well-off in society" (Talisse: 50). This view, based on fairness doctrine, was supportive of such public policy as affirmative action in the United States to correct past injustices based on racial discrimination in society. Yet Rawls's view, in terms of Berlin's two concepts of liberty, though it leaned in the direction of "positive" liberty remained on the whole oriented to the notion of freedom in the individualist sense.

But the critics of Rawls pointed to the incompleteness of his argument for justice viewed narrowly from the individualist perspective. One critic of non-European (Tamil) origin observed:

In a world of moral and cultural diversity one of the subjects over which there is dispute, and even conflict, is the subject of justice. Different peoples, or groups, or communities, have different views or conceptions of justice. In these circumstances the question is: how can people live together freely when there is this sort of moral diversity? One kind of answer suggests that the solution is to articulate a conception of justice that is capable of commanding widespread, if not universal, assent. But the problem with this move is that, in order to secure that assent, it is necessary to strip the conception of justice of much of its substantive content or run the risk of having a theory which commands the loyalty of only a small subset of its audience. Yet stripped of too much of its substantive content it ceases to be a theory of justice at all (Kukathas: 6).

Since Rawls's formulation about justice, hence good society, presupposes the liberal order, therefore, according to critics, it is exclusionary of those other formulations of justice that are based on other conceptions of political order. It follows that liberal order is one sort of order in a pluralist world where other arrangements exist and are legitimate based on their premises. The argument for acknowledging diversity essentially rests on the view that an individual is a creature of his society and carries with him the markings or imprints of his culture. In this view the original sin of liberalism was to strip the individual of his cultural imprints in order to construct the imagined individual as man standing outside of or prior to society, hence culture, to which he belonged. Thus in re-opening the debate on the moral philosophy and politics of liberalism by means of his theory of justice and in the subsequent response to his critics in *Political Liberalism*, Rawls unintentionally offered the sorely needed space to construct from within the grounds of liberalism a theory or justification of multiculturalism.

At the heart of liberalism, it has been said, there is a hole since liberal theory does not take into account group identity.[4] This is the hole the theory of multiculturalism attempts to fill. The fairness doctrine is viewed by Rawls's critics as incomplete and inadequate if it fails a large portion of individuals in society whose sense of self-worth and dignity are based on group identity, or whose cultures originate outside of the shared cultural system of liberal societies. Social justice requires equality of treatment be available for everyone in society without presupposition, and extending recognition, as Charles Taylor advocates, to groups, immigrant cultural communities and indigenous populations of first nations, would help make the half-empty vessel of fairness doctrine reasonably full. Bhiku Parekh observed in assessing the work of Rawls, that the liberal society he conceived "does not leave enough space for diversity" (2000: 90). Multiculturalism then is offered as the positive cure of the shortcoming of liberalism, and not its replacement. In this view it is an opening to and embracing of the crowded world that is immensely diverse, of acknowledging the cultural embeddedness of human beings, of encouraging intercultural dialogue as the means of building a more harmonious liberal and democratic society where all existing cultural groups are equally recognized and equally treated, and that such a multicultural society holds out the promise of developing a new sense of solidarity that is not based on ethnicity or religion or any one ideological doctrine but, instead, is "political in nature and based on a shared commitment to the political community" (ibid: 336-341).

---

[4] F. Fukuyama, "Identity, Immigration, and Liberal Democracy," *Journal of Democracy*, 17, 2 (April, 2006), pp. 5-20.

Chapter Three

MULTICULTURALISM, IMMIGRATION & CITIZENSHIP

Human migration in search of better climate, pasture for herding and land for sowing, resource for hunting and building, escape from natural disasters and man-made conflicts is older than recorded history. In our times technical arguments and theoretical approaches describing as "push" and "pull" factors for explaining human migration do not alter the basic urge behind the movement of people across great distances and nature's barriers from the remotest past.

We are concerned here with migration in the age of nation-states with border controls, and every reasonable effort of states depending on their capacity to monitor and prohibit free movements of people across international political boundaries. Under these circumstances we cannot speak of human migration — irrespective of the "push" and "pull" factors at work in the movement of people in search for economic pay-off or fleeing from natural disasters, famines and wars — as *free* movement of people. The sort of migration that populated the *New* World (Americas and Australia) from the *Old* World (Europe) practically ended with the First World War. In the post-1945 period the trend in migration shifted to movement of people from the *Third* World (non-European countries and former European colonies in Asia, Africa, the Caribbean basin and South America) to the *First* World (advanced industrial societies of Europe, North America and Australia). This accelerating shift in migration since the late 1960s has provided the context and impetus in which the argument in favour of multiculturalism was advanced in Canada and other liberal-democracies in the West.

II.

In order to appreciate the nature and effect of what might be termed the "second wave" of migration beginning at about the mid-point of the last century, it will be useful to briefly review the "big picture" on the subject. I am indebted in sketching this big picture to the work of Jeffrey G. Williamson and the figures on mass migration he compiled. In *The Political Economy of World Mass Migration*, Williamson writes:

The first global century took place between about 1820 and World War I, characterized by falling barriers to trade and to the flows of labor and capital. All three boomed. Since about 1950, the second global century has tried to reintegrate these three markets in the wake of the interwar autarchic retreat (2005: 1).

Williamson's reference to the "first global century" in modern history, during which period numbers involved in mass migration might be estimated, also coincided with the first century of liberalism in England that A.J.P. Taylor described as the example of a liberal country. The two world wars and the great depression of the last century greatly ruptured the process of liberalization of the global economy, and put a halt to mass migration accompanying that process from the Old World to the New (the United States, Canada, Australia, Argentina and Brazil). Williamson's study is mainly focused on figures derived from public records and earlier studies of migration by American researchers for the United States.

The combined effects of wars and economic dislocation in the first half of the last century meant, as Williamson indicates, the United States by 1950s "was no longer a melting pot or a nation of immigrants but rather a closed economy whose youth was mostly native born" (ibid: 26). Just prior to the start of World War I immigration into the United States, primarily from Europe, exceeded one million in 1913 and in 1914; at the end of the war the figures for 1918 and 1919 were 60,000 and 54,000 respectively. Following economic recovery there was a short-lived spike in immigration from overseas reaching the level set during the period 1885-1900. This brief spurt dissolved under the weight of the Great Depression and then World War II. Williamson writes:

The average between 1922 and 1929 was 232,000, a figure about one-third the 1881-1914 average. During the Great Depression decade, the flood dried up to a trickle, averaging about 50,000 each year. The great mass migration was over (ibid: 28).

The comparative figures for overseas immigration to Canada (provided by Canada Employment and Immigration Services, and compiled for the years 1852-1986 in Freda Hawkins's impressive and definitive study of immigration to Canada) during this period are similar to that of the United States, though in percentage terms the Canadian figures are higher given the difference in the total population of the two countries. For instance, the figures for 1912 and 1913 were 375,756 and 400,870; towards the end of the war the figures for 1917 and 1918 were 72,910 and 41,845. In the period 1919-30 overseas immigration reached an average of 120,000, and then collapsed for the period 1931-1950 to an average of 33,000 (Hawkins: 402).

After 1950 mass migration, increasingly from the Third World countries to the First World, steadily rose in numbers reaching an annual figure of over a million in the 1990s. Though the average number of immigrants amounted to similar figures reached a century earlier, yet the absolute numbers were smaller in proportion to the population of the destination country. According to Williamson:

The U.S. annual immigration rate fell from 11.6 immigrants per thousand in the 1900s to 0.4 immigrant per thousand in the 1940s, before rising again to 4 immigrants per thousand in the 1990s. The proportion of the U.S. population born in a foreign land had fallen from a 1910 peak of 15 percent to an all-century low of 4.7 percent in 1970. The postwar immigration boom increased the foreign-born share to more than 8 percent in 1990 and more than 10 percent in 2000. Thus, the United States has come two-thirds of the way back to reclaiming the title "a nation of immigrants" after a half-century retreat (2005: 1-2).

Similarly, new arrivals at an average of 156,000 annually in the 1950s represented growth in immigration to Canada (Hawkins: 402). The average was somewhat distorted by the huge spike for the year 1957 following the Suez and Hungarian crises of 1956 which swelled the ranks of new arrivals (ibid: 74). During the three decades 1951-81 Canada accepted some 4.4 million immigrants as the total population increased from 15.4 million to 20.2 million (ibid: 401). In terms of the percentage of foreign (mostly of European origin) to native born, the composition of Canada's population remained stable around 20 percent in the period 1931-81 from a high of 28 percent for the decade 1901-11 (ibid).

These figures for the United States and Canada show that the numbers of immigrants in percentage term arriving annually in the "second global century" beginning in 1950 remained below the peak reached during the "first global century" of mass migration. What does stand out, however, for the period 1965-2000 is the increase in the percentage of foreign-born relative to host country's total population rising from 6 percent to 13 percent in North America, and this also indicated the shift that has taken place in the source of immigrants from the Old World to the Third World countries.

In respect to the source-area composition of immigrants to the United States, during the period 1951-60 more than half the immigrants originated from Europe, nearly 40 percent were from the Americas (and of this figure a quarter were from Mexico), and some 6 percent were of Asian origin with less than 1 percent from Africa (Williamson: 4). In contrast, the figures for 1991-2000 showed a sharp decline for immigrants from Europe amounting to 15 percent of the total; the figures for immigrants from Americas increased to nearly 50 percent of which half came from Mexico. But there was a five-fold jump to over 30 percent of the total for immigrants arriving from Asia; the number for immigrants from Africa also rose sharply to nearly 4 percent of the total (ibid). The figures for Canada, as provided by Statistics Canada, are comparable to that of the United States. In the period before 1961 over 90 percent of immigrants to Canada were of European origin and barely 3 percent came from Asia. In the period 1991-2001 immigrants of European origin arriving in Canada declined to below 20 percent of the total arrivals and the percentage of Asian immigrants soared to above 58 percent. The figures for the same period for immigrants from Africa, and from the Caribbean, Central and South America were 7.6 percent and 10.9 percent respectively (Statistics Canada: 39).

The dramatic shift in the source-area composition of immigrants into North America (Canada and the United States) might be explained primarily by the changes in the political and economic situations in Europe and Asia. The devastations of the Second World War created the situation for Europeans to seek security through immigration in the two decades immediately following the end of the war. As Europe recovered and political conditions stabilized there was less incentive for migration. The political and economic situation in Asia, on the contrary, went into a downward spiral with wars, revolutions, civil strife and impoverished economy during the period of surge in Asian immigration into North America. A secondary explanation would be that the effects of globalization came to be increasingly felt in the same period of surge in Asian immigration, and one of the main features of globalization that pushed this surge was the revolution in the modes of transportation and communication during the second half of the last century.

III.

The "second wave" of mass migration beginning in the 1950s needs to be distinguished from the "first wave" during the first global century that Williamson describes. The "first wave" of migration to the New World was made up of mostly immigrants of European origin, including Jews escaping from persecution and anti-Semitic bigotry in Europe. The "second wave" of migration is increasingly made up of immigrants from the Third World, and the context of globalization in which this migration is occurring sets it apart from the "first wave" of migration in the period 1820-1914. Consequently, what is required to explain the difference is a sort of "sociology of immigration" to take into account how globalization has affected migration, and what has been its social and political effects for advanced liberal democracies of the West.

In 1958 John Kennedy, then a U.S. Senator from Massachusetts, published a small book titled *A Nation of Immigrants*.

As Robert Kennedy noted in his preface to the 1964 revised edition of the book following President Kennedy's assassination, it was written to remind Americans of the history of migration in the making of the United States and the contributions of immigrants to their adopted country. But there was also the more compelling proximate political reason for writing the book; this was connected to the reform of the immigration system which John Kennedy supported. President Kennedy wanted to see an open-door immigration policy with an end to the quota system and the elimination of discrimination based on national (ethnic) origins of those seeking to migrate to the United States. In 1963 President Kennedy wrote to the Congress:

The use of a national origins system is without basis in either logic or reason. It neither satisfies a national need nor accomplishes an international purpose. In an age of interdependence among nations, such a system is an anachronism, for it discriminates among applicants for admission into the United States on the basis of accident of birth (1964: 149).

Two years after the tragic death of President Kennedy the Immigration and Nationality Act of 1965 was passed. It abolished quotas based on national-origins and opened the door to immigration on the basis of family reunification. It was also in keeping with the politics of the Cold War, which required denying the former Soviet Union influence among developing countries of the Third World at the expense of the West, and the need for low-wage workers given the demand of post-1945 expanding economies in Europe and North America.

Canadian response in policy terms was not much different from that of the United States in the 1950s. Ottawa began to put in place the administrative mechanism required to manage the flow of immigrants and a selection process for people wanting to come to Canada. Any effort to put some constraints on the claims made by prospective immigrants on the grounds of family re-unification was deemed politically unacceptable, and under this scheme the steady flow of immigrants has continued. The preference for national origins of applicants favouring Europeans over people of colour was replaced by preference given to educational and vocational skills in keeping with the demand for labour in a growing economy.

There is a difference, however, in the attitude of Canadians to immigration and immigrants, as Freda Hawkins has pointed out, in the making of the country from that of the Americans. In the United States the story of immigration and immigrants has been woven into the fabric of the country's history as its foundational narrative. This is transparent in President Kennedy's book, *A Nation of Immigrants*, celebrating the history of immigration as the defining element in the sort of country the United States became. But in Canada the story of immigrants and immigration neither constitutes the foundational narrative of Canadian history, nor is it viewed as central to the making and advancement of the country. Instead, the central fact of Canadian history is "the existence of two founding races and the relationship between them" (Hawkins: 34). Yet despite this difference the policy of open-door immigration in the United States and Canada that came into force in the 1960s — Canada's centennial decade — did not take into account how the revolution in transportation would alter the meaning of migration in the new circumstances of the increasing interdependence of nations which President Kennedy alluded to in his support for a new immigration statute.

Air travel in the years between the two world wars of the last century was a harbinger of things to come and, especially, of how greatly it would impact upon the movement of people in the "second wave" of migration. Until the arrival of air travel migration from the Old World to the New was an ordeal that required of those leaving their native land for unknown prospects the sort of temperament and commitment needed to surmount the hazards of the journey. The revolution in transportation would affect the nature of migration, and what it would mean for host countries receiving new arrivals. Hence, in our world of globalization with people on the move as never before, we need to consider whether the words "immigrant" and "immigration" mean the same today as they did before the 1960s when the arrival of wide-body aircrafts dramatically changed the nature of long-distance travel.

In the normal or traditional sense an immigrant is an individual departing his native country to settle permanently in an intended host country, and adopt the customs and values of the host country while giving it his full loyalty. Migration during the "first wave" and into the early years of the "second wave" in the 1950s involved considerable expense for travel by way of trains and ships over many weeks. The decision to make the journey required psychological preparation on the part of immigrants in both leaving their native land with some certainty of never returning, and of anticipating the new country with challenges ahead of settlement and assimilation. Immigration meant cutting one's ties with the past in preparation of entering a new world for the future. An immigrant was mostly brimming with gratitude on arriving in the country of his choice and grateful for the opportunities open to him that did not exist or were denied him in the land of his birth.

Kennedy wrote movingly about the perils that confronted immigrants, and of how the journey itself contributed to transforming an immigrant leaving behind the Old World into an eagerly embracing citizen of the New World. In this sense, the experience of immigrants arriving in the United States was about the same as those making it to Canada. Here is how Kennedy described the perils and the challenges for immigrants to the New World:

Eventually the journey came to an end. The travelers saw the coast of America with mixed feelings of relief, excitement, trepidation and anxiety. For now, uprooted from old patterns of life, they found themselves in [Oscar] Handlin's phrase, "in a prolonged state of crisis — crisis in the sense that they were, and remained, unsettled." They reached the new land exhausted by lack of rest, bad food, confinement and the strain of adjustment to new conditions. But they could not pause to recover their strength. They had no reserves of food or money; they had to keep moving until they found work. This meant new strains at a time when their capacity to cope with new problems had already been overburdened (1964: 24).

But the future was one of hope, and accompanying hope was the feeling of gratitude. Again Kennedy:

In the community he had left, the immigrant usually had a fixed place. He would carry on his father's craft or trade; he would farm his father's land, or that small portion of it that was left to him after it was divided with his brothers. Only with the most exceptional talent and enterprise could he break out of the mold in which life had cast him. There was no such mold for him in the New World. Once having broken with the past, except for sentimental ties and cultural inheritance, he had to rely on his own abilities. It was the future and not the past to which he was compelled to address himself. Except for the Negro slave, he could go anywhere and do anything his talents permitted. A sprawling continent lay before him, and he had only to weld it together by canals, by railroads and by roads. If he failed to achieve the dream for himself, he could still retain it for his children (ibid: 27).

Out of such commitments and sentiments immigrants arriving in the New World from the Old embraced the host country, which they adopted as their own and to which they gave more often than not their unreserved gratitude and loyalty.

The wide-body aircraft that came into use in the late 1960s very rapidly altered the meaning of transcontinental and transoceanic travel in terms of time and cost required to traverse distances. The world became increasingly a smaller place since the 1960s as the economy of travel became dramatically more egalitarian. The cost of traveling declined despite the oil-shocks of 1973-74, 1979 and the steadily rising fuel prices in the final two decades of the last century.

The transportation revolution blurred the difference between immigrants and migrant workers. A migrant worker, in contrast to an immigrant, remains situated in two countries: his native home and his place of work. He does not make the same choices as does an immigrant, and the host country does not also require of him the sort of commitment it requires of an immigrant since his presence is considered temporary. Migrant workers are not a new phenomenon, although globalization has spurred the demand for and supply of migrant workers. An example of this phenomenon is the presence of a large population of migrant workers in the oil-producing states of the Persian Gulf.

The situation of migrant workers becomes a sticky one when the host country admits them, and allows them to remain permanently as immigrants. This is what has been taking place in Europe and North America with the rise in the "second wave" mass migration from the Third World to the First World. Over the past 40 years the consequences arising from failed and near-failed states in Asia, Africa, the Caribbean basin, Central and South America have resulted in a surge of migrants seeking economic opportunities in the First World countries. The transportation revolution that preceded this surge in mass migration has been instrumental in shaping the movement of people, and conditioning their expectations. This revolution made it possible for an individual in Asia or Africa, for example, to have breakfast in Karachi or Cairo and look for dinner in New York City or Toronto on arrival the same day. The flip side of this new circumstance of reduced travel time to a fraction of what earlier generations of "first wave" immigrants took in reaching their destination is that immigrants and migrant workers are only a few short hours removed from their native lands. The journey from the Old World to the New across oceans on ships was an act laden with the practicality and the symbol of breaking ties with the land of one's birth; in the journey from the Third World to the First there was no more such breaking of ties required, nor would it carry similar psychological effect as it did for earlier generations of immigrants, as distance became reduced to mere inconvenience of journey between two points on a greatly time-shrunken world of air travel.

According to a 2004 UN study, the number of international migrants more than doubled in the period 1970-2000 (Koser: 5). The global figure for migrants in 1970 was 81.5 million, and by 2000 the number of migrants around the world increased to nearly 175 million; by 2005 it was estimated the figure exceeded 200 million migrants around the world. The number of migrants living in the developed world (First World countries) nearly tripled from 38.3 million in 1970 to 110.3 million in 2000. During the same period the number of migrants within the developing world (Third World countries) rose from 43.2 million in 1970 to 64.6 million in 2000 (ibid). The huge pressure these numbers bring on the need for some permanent settlement of those leaving their native countries for economic opportunities, or driven by wars and natural calamities, can only be alleviated by the absorptive capacity of host countries in the West and in particular by Canada, the United States and Australia.

But in the milieu of multiculturalism the absorption of such large numbers of migrant workers into liberal democracies of the West poses the sort of problem that "first wave" immigrants never did. Open-immigration at first was received with a sense of novelty. But there was also the fear of those who anticipated eventually the culture and politics of host countries could be irreversibly damaged. Among those who voiced such concerns the most notable was the British parliamentarian Enoch Powell. At a Conservative Party gathering in Birmingham on April 20, 1968, Powell warned how unrestricted immigration was inexorably and unalterably changing the nature of British society. More than four decades later Powell's speech is remembered only for what was then considered inflammatory by his peers. But for Powell it was about numbers as he stated, "bearing in mind that numbers are of the essence: the significance and consequences of an alien element introduced into a country or population are profoundly different according to whether that element is 1 per cent or 10 per cent" (1991: 373-79). The Birmingham speech ended for Powell a distinguished political career as his warnings went unheeded, and he was removed from the Conservative's shadow cabinet. In the aftermath of July 2005 suicide bombings in London, and concerns over "homegrown terror" from radicalized Muslim immigrants or Muslims born in Britain, Powell's warning in retrospect was prophetic for contemporary Britain and the West in general. Afsun Qureshi-Smith, a Pakistani-Canadian writer residing in Britain, on the basis of her own childhood recollection has described from the inside the tensions or contradictions that surround migrant workers who never fully embraced their adopted country as immigrants. She writes:

I can only speak from experience, and here it is. As a child, my parents had no specific interest in the Canadian culture and were deeply entrenched in their own insular world: Indo/Pakistani friends, food, music, etc. There were — briefly — a couple of white friends, one even Jewish, but in a short time they let these people go for a myriad of reasons (they required alcohol, they didn't speak the language, they didn't like our food). After that, the people who came into our household were all friends in the community or relatives — all Sunnis, and all Indian/Pakistanis.

Growing up, I may as well have been in Hyderabad or Karachi. I asked my parents all the time — why did you immigrate? Why didn't you go back? I usually got some grumbling about the heat and the filth, and the great medical treatment here.

And that is what irks me. My parents came to the Western world and led a better life, but they didn't integrate or ever aspire to. They were the poster immigrants for the Trudeau era, except that their community didn't slot itself in the mosaic as Trudeau so ardently wanted. In fact, looking back, my parents probably should have just gone back home.[5]

---

[5] Afsun Qureshi-Smith, "Fundamentalists, go home," *National Post*, November 16, 2010.

The unwillingness of host countries in the West to distinguish between an immigrant and a migrant worker has meant extending the same political and social benefits to both. In processing their official papers the host countries have extended to migrant workers the same privileges of citizenship that allow them to reside as immigrants earning income that was for them the "pull" factor in bringing them to depart from their native countries without having to cut ties, and to live a life of divided loyalties or, worse, of drawing social and economic benefits from the host country while nurturing an animus toward it because of political loyalties to another country or culture or ideology. This unwillingness to distinguish between immigrants and migrant workers — between those who sought to embrace the West and did on arrival, and those who came seeking economic and social benefits as migrant workers without any wish to embrace the West — has reached an absurd level when host countries in the West readily provide welfare to those, such as radical Muslim priests and Islamists, who brazenly ridicule and preach hatred for liberal democracy and the culture of freedom that separates the West from the cultures of the East and, in particular, the world of Islam.

IV.

In our contemporary world globalization, pushed by revolutions in communication and transportation, has brought about high mobility of people and even higher mobility of capital while also increasing the interdependence of states. The result of such changes has unsettled politics just about everywhere. Politics most simply stated, and therefore much left unstated, is the organized response of people to manage their affairs within the bounded space of the country they call their own. Globalization and interdependence have meant no country can any longer remain closed to the outside world and resist pressures of change brought to bear on established norms, rules, customs and traditions by which people have conducted their affairs for some time. Ironically countries most pressed to accommodate demands for change are those which are also most open to the world, most respectful of individual rights in theory and in practice, most evolved or mature in the rule of democracy or, in other words, liberal democracies of the West.

One subject on which pressure for change has been felt as a result of open-door immigration and the movement of people from the Third World to the First World countries is in the meaning of citizenship. Invariably open door immigration means the profile of the population in the host country is going to change over time as is occurring in Canada, and with that change the inescapable question looming ever larger remains how much of that change will affect politics. Ever since Aristotle (384-322 B.C.), "people" refer to, in the context of politics, to those living together within a politically organized entity, a state, and sharing a common set of values. The cumulative effect of globalization and immigration putting under pressure shared common values within liberal democracies is undeniable as recent history illustrates with demands on host countries to accommodate the cultural values and norms of the new immigrants. This has meant re-negotiating the meaning of citizenship with far reaching consequences for politics in liberal democracies.

Citizenship means membership and belonging. This is succinctly stated in a recent study as follows, "Membership lies at the heart of citizenship. To be a citizen is to belong to a given political community" (Bellamy: 52). In just about every culture an individual is nurtured by a sense of membership in and belonging to the community into which he is born, but every culture historically speaking did not possess the idea of citizenship as it has evolved since it was originally articulated in Athens, Greece, in the fifth century B.C. In other words, the idea of citizenship though universally adopted for the identity of membership in and belonging to a sovereign and independent political community, the state, is by origin a western idea and influenced by the specific conditions of political developments of the West, first in ancient Greece and then in modern history specifically following the two revolutions of the eighteenth century in the making of republican democracies of the United States and France. In both instances, despite the twists and turns of history over centuries, the common elements implied in the idea of citizenship were that *free* individuals together constituted a political community that was a *democracy*.

In Book III of *Politics* Aristotle famously provided the definition of citizen and classifications of governments by types: *good types* — monarchy, aristocracy, and constitutional commonwealth;

bad types — tyranny, oligarchy, and extreme democracy. He wrote of the citizen as an individual who "shares in the administration of justice and in offices" (1943: 287). There were qualifications surrounding citizenship in Aristotle's description, but the definition he provided was "best adapted to the citizens of a democracy" (ibid: 288). While Aristotle considered democracy a perversion of constitutional commonwealth, government in such an arrangement belonged to the many in contrast to the few in an aristocracy and one in a monarchy. The well-being of constitutional government rested in his view on the "virtues of a citizen" which required a good citizen knowing "how to govern like a freeman, and how to obey like a freeman" (ibid: 292). Aristotle summarized, "The conception of the citizen now begins to clear up. He who has the power to take part in the deliberative or judicial administration of any state is said by us to be a citizen of that state. And speaking generally, a state is a body of citizens sufficing for the purposes of life" (ibid: 288).

A state and its government administered by the many for the common good of all of its inhabitants, as Aristotle discussed, was the celebrated Athens of Pericles in the fifth century B.C. that Thucydides (460-400 B.C.) described in his *History* of the Peloponessian war. Pericles's eulogy of his native Athens has been immortalized in Thucydides's account, and it was that description of Athenian politics that Aristotle likely thought about in his discussion of constitutional government. Pericles noted, "Our constitution is called a democracy because power is in the hands not of a minority but of the whole people" (Thucydides: 145). Many centuries later Abraham Lincoln's elegantly simple definition of democracy as "government of the people, by the people, for the people" given in his Gettysburg Address of November 19, 1863 echoed the words of Pericles from around 430 B.C. The sort of people who understood the principle and mechanics of such state and government, and then defended them tended to be, as Pericles praised Athenians of his time, "free and tolerant in our private lives; but in public affairs we keep to the law. This is because it commands our deep respect" (ibid: 145). And again, such people knew "happiness depends on being free, and freedom depends on being courageous" (ibid: 149-150).

From Aristotle we know that democracy was not broadly favoured as the best or most desirable form of government. But in Pericles's praise of Athenian society, as reported in or constructed by

Thucydides, the virtue of democracy and requirements of its citizens as first principles were for the very first time stated and have remained valid since then. A free people are politically equal irrespective of naturally born differences among them, and only a constitution deliberated and devised by representatives of free people could have their consent. In such a political community the mechanics of government requires the participation in offices and representation through elections of the free people. A citizen in democracy, as Pericles spoke about and Aristotle discussed in his *Politics*, is a free individual and citizenship has meant the rights, duties and obligations of a citizen to his political community. A modern chronicler of democracy, in reflecting on what such an arrangement amounted to in political life, writes:

For Pericles, as Thucydides makes him speak, the democracy of Athens was a way of living together in political freedom, which ennobled the characters and refined the sensibilities of an entire community. It opened up to them lives rich with interest and gratification, and protected them effectively in living out these lives with one another. It would be hard sanely to ask for more from any set of political institutions or practices (Dunn: 28).

Athenian democracy did not survive, but the ideas it gave birth to survived the Roman Republic and the Roman Empire to influence political thought in the making of the modern world.

Two millennia later the subject of citizenship in practical terms re-emerged in the American Revolution of 1776 and the French Revolution of 1789. In the years before these two revolutions inaugurated the modern world of politics based on the idea of democracy, political philosophers struggled with the varying tensions between the notions of political and legal equality of people within a sovereign state. The English philosophers Hobbes and Locke in their own respective ways reconciled the issue of political and legal equality through the doctrine of the consent of free individuals recognizing the rule of a just sovereign. The consent stood for a social contract entered into by free people to form a state and acceptance of the rule of law as binding. The political and legal thinking that went into the general idea of social contract was a theoretical construct, and yet it served a purpose. As Sir Ernest Barker explained, "it [social contract theory] was none the less a way of expressing two fundamental ideas or values to which the human mind will always cling — the value of Liberty, or the idea that will, not force, is the basis of government, and the value of Justice, or the idea that right, not might, is the basis of all political society and of every system of political order" (1960: viii). Jefferson, the author of the American Declaration of Independence, advanced the view as did some others in his time such as Thomas Paine in *Common Sense* that free people are obliged to annul their social contract by withdrawing consent to be ruled by an unjust sovereign. This was the basis of the American Revolution, as it would be of the French Revolution, and the idea of sovereignty embodied in a living monarch would get transferred to "We, the People of the United States" in the case of America, and "the source of all sovereignty lies essentially in the Nation" in the case of France (Bellamy: 42). In this manner the two revolutions merged the old tension between political and legal equality going all the way back to the Athenian democracy and the Roman Empire in the idea of citizenship of free and equal individuals of a constitutionally governed democracy.

The two eighteenth century revolutions, American and French, prioritized freedom ahead of democracy or the nature of government. The logic was simple, that only free people could form and participate in government that would be fair and equitable. Since then citizenship in modern liberal-democracy has meant freedom and equality inherent in individuals give them the right as well as the obligation to participate through elections in the affairs of the government and state. Citizenship moreover, as noted, has meant membership and belonging; membership in state comes either through the natural rights of birth or through naturalization, and belonging has meant exclusive attachment with and loyalty to one particular political community.

In recent years this notion of exclusive membership and belonging which citizenship came to mean has been subject to systematic criticism, and demands to make citizenship more inclusive and flexible by making it open and available to people made stateless, or refugees, for no fault of their own as a result of wars, natural calamities and the phenomenon of failed states, and to migrants in search of economic opportunities (Bellamy: chapter 8). In whatever manner the meaning of citizenship is re-negotiated in modern liberal democracies, it needs to be understood that the concept of citizenship is a core component of modernity. Modernity has multiple meanings or dimensions: industrialization, urbanization, the spread and adoption of liberal values, women and minority rights, elected representative governments, etc., and among these is citizenship. The advancement of this idea has meant that even though society is a collection of individuals, individual rights override collective rights based on tribal or group identity and distinguish modern society from mob rule. On this idea rests the modern liberal democratic society where political leaders are elected by citizens to whom they are accountable. They hold office with citizen approval; they make laws, but none might be passed that override the unalienable rights of citizens written into the constitution. They govern with support of the citizens and are replaced when they fail to meet the goals that saw them elected.

The workings of a modern liberal democratic society, its stability and its prosperity, require a citizenry educated in the ideals of democracy and joined together in defending those ideals expressed through its institutions. A citizenry divided over the nature and ideals of liberal democracy imperils it from within. A successful liberal democracy is the political construction of its citizenry spanning across generations, and the citizens reflect in the manner of their living the culture of democracy that is markedly different from those cultures that have not been shaped from within by political ideas based on the principle of individual liberty. Democracy eventually is a culture embracing politics, religion, history and society in a certain arrangement that happens to be markedly different from other systems, such as aristocracy, that Tocqueville discovered in his journey through America. According to George Kateb, a contemporary political philosopher, the cluster of values distinguishing democratic culture from non-democratic culture is qualitative. "In its distinctive way of forming political authority," Kateb observed, "representative democracy cultivates distinctive ways of acting in nonpolitical life — of seeking and giving, of making claims for oneself and one's group and acknowledging the claims of others" (1992: 43). The challenge, therefore, for liberal democracy is domestic and internal in an increasingly interdependent world of nations and cultures. It arises from competing demands of different cultural groups for equal recognition, when such demands invariably generate divisions among its citizenry, within the political boundaries of a liberal democratic society.

Chapter Four

TWISTING OUR HISTORY

The modern democratic age turned history into an arena of intense and often divisive contest over recalling the past. History is about the past remembered, or in the words of historian John Lukacs "the remembered past," which informs us as to who we are and how our present was shaped by events and forces at play before our time. The eminent historian Margaret MacMillan in *The Uses and Abuses of History* notes, "History is about remembering the past but it is also about what we choose to forget" (2009: 127). The increasing intensity of this contest is in part reflective of what is at stake, the memory recalled and the identity of a people constructed or imagined that are then used to legitimate political demands. It might be said historians were never entirely neutral about their subjects; what makes, however, history increasingly divisive in the democratic age is the extent to which it is served or used in the political arena for advancing special interests of race, class and gender disguised as public interest, and contesting what were once broadly held views about past events and individuals who lived in different times and different circumstances.

Alexis de Tocqueville, in writing about America, noted the shift in sentiments over history with the making of the democratic age. Tocqueville observed historians writing in "aristocratic centuries" dwelled on the role of great individuals. This is because when "they cast their eyes on the theater of the world, they perceive first of all a very few principal actors who guide the whole play" (2000: 469). In contrast, the concerns of the democratic age driven by the politics of equality "brings the human mind to search for the general reason that could strike so many intellects at once and turn them simultaneously in the same direction" (ibid: 470). The search for "general reason" expressed in terms of impersonal forces — for instance, social, economic, technological or demographic variable — as arbiter of our history has contributed to what Margaret MacMillan describes as "history wars." Since history is primarily about the past remembered and our collective memory, or *Je me souviens* as the Quebec automobile license plate proclaims, the "general reason" tends to be what may appeal to the contemporary public. MacMillan writes:

Some of the most difficult and protracted wars in societies around the world have been over what is being omitted or downplayed in the telling of their history — and what should be in. When people talk, as they frequently do, about the need for "proper" history, what they really mean is the history they want and like. School textbooks, university courses, movies, books, war memorials, art galleries, and museums have all from time to time been caught in debates that say as much or more about the present and its concerns as they do about the ostensible subject of history (2009: 127).

These "history wars" of our times are over what is remembered and what is deliberately left out; of the extent to which politics dictates what sort of history should be written and taught. History ironically then becomes the trimming and selling of the past to the public, and the public "taste" for history then tends to get shaped by present needs and prevailing prejudices.

What MacMillan has written about "history wars" was vividly illustrated in the politics surrounding the commemoration of the two hundred and fiftieth anniversary of the Battle of Quebec, September 13, 1759, fought between the English and French armies on the Plains of Abraham. The defeat of French forces under General Marquis de Montcalm by the English soldiers led by Major-General James Wolfe was one of the defining moments in the making of Canada as a Dominion under the British crown. But for the present-day Quebec nationalists that long ago event has a bitter taste, its memory to be squelched or remembered only as humiliation that requires reversal by securing independence for the French-speaking Quebec nation from the rest of Canada. French-Canadian or Quebec nationalist/separatist opposition to commemorating the Battle of Quebec meant scrapping any official event recalling this significant occasion in the history of Canada. According to one journalist, "A re-enactment on the Plains of

Abraham was hustled off stage earlier this year when noisy Quebec nationalists complained. There's a Canada Post stamp for the 100th anniversary of the little-known Boundary Waters Treaty with the U.S., but not one to note the 250th anniversary of the Battle of Quebec. If not for the provocative reading of the FLQ manifesto at the battlefield this weekend, the significance of Sept. 13, 1759, might not be marked at all."[6]

The "history wars," as in this instance of the controversy surrounding whether to officially commemorate or not an event of decisive importance in the subsequent making of Canada, indicate how greatly political sentiments of the day trim and shape our understanding of history. This is not uncommon, and this play of politics and history in a deeper sense is paradoxically indicative also of what makes for the difference between liberal democracy open to the push and pull of public opinion and non-democracy or illiberal democracy.

But in the absence or weakening of a common understanding of a nation's history, warts and all, there arises the inevitable fractures among the people about who they are and what are their shared commitments in the well-being of their country. Such fractures if not repaired over time can only get wider and threaten the dissolution of the country as has happened so many times — too many to recall here, such as the break-up of Czechoslovakia peacefully in January 1993 or the breaking apart of Pakistan as a result of civil war and mass killings in December 1971 — around the world.

When the minority Conservative government of Prime Minister Stephen Harper on November 22, 2006 tabled the motion in the House of Commons recognizing Quebec as a nation within Canada, there was near unanimity among the members on both sides of the aisle in supporting it. The motion was symbolic, but symbols matter and Mr. Harper's intent was to give symbolic recognition to Quebec as a nation with separate language and distinct culture that has been its demand for a long time; yet fear that this gesture instead of healing the country's politics might unravel it was not assuaged. The discordant note on the motion was sounded outside the parliament by a large number of Canadians opposed to it according to a poll done by

---

[6] Peter S. Taylor, "The French were never going to win," *National Post*, September 11, 2009.

Leger Marketing. This poll showed the country divided about equally in the Canada-wide survey with 48 percent in support of the Conservative motion and 47 percent opposed.[7] Following the parliamentary passage of the motion the widely read Anglophone journalist, Andrew Coyne, plaintively asked, "who will defend, not just the unity of the country, but its integrity; who will uphold a meaningful role for the federal government, as the only government of all the people; who will speak of *Canada* as a nation."[8]

The recognition of Quebec as a nation might be defended as good politics, yet it also weakened an understanding of the history of Canada that speaks to the idea of one *Canadian* nation. The "history wars" invariably become a zero-sum game of competing "national" or "ethnic" interests as has happened within Canada. This was Trudeau's view, and he expressed it in his own style when invited to address the Senate in March 1988 in the midst of the national debate over the 1987 Meech Lake Accord that recognized Quebec constitutionally as a "distinct society" within Canada. In recalling a "statement of principles for a new constitution" that he presented to the parliament in 1977 which began with the words "We, the people of Canada," Trudeau said:

I think it was pretty hard to beat, but, look, it was panned by the English-speaking columnists, and do you want to know what happened in Quebec? It did not get beyond the fifth word. When we said, "We, the people of Canada," one hullabaloo broke out in Quebec...

So there was one great scandal, because we started the preamble with the words, "We, the people of Canada." The outrage of not only Premier Levesque but of Quebec intelligentsia and the Quebec media was enormous. Somehow we could not even talk about the people of Canada (Hansard, 1988).

"History wars" have made of Canada a divided country, and the divisions have become more accentuated since the centennial year. The motion on Quebec passed by the federal parliament in November 2006 was not greeted with an overwhelming support of the country; it

---

[7] CanWest News Service, "Quebec 'nation' debate divides French, English," in www.canada.com, November 11, 2006.
[8] A. Coyne, "Quebec the elephant at Liberal convention," AndrewCoyne.com, November 29, 2006.

did not heal existing divisions; it obscured, instead, the reality of that aspect of Canadian history which spoke to the efforts of past generations in striving to overcome the racial and ethnic divide at the country's origin. One Canadian expressed his dismay in these words: "Whether it was the alliance of French and English reformers who fought to bring democracy to the colonies in 1848, or the bicultural partnership that achieved Confederation in 1867, or the sacrifices of 5,000 or more Canadian francophones who died in the service of their country in two world wars, the most ennobling work of our nation has been to join the different cultures that emerged out of two of history's great empires in a single civic enterprise" (Griffiths: 9-10). But multiculturalism — the celebration in keeping with Canada's *official* policy that the diverse cultures of immigrants are all inherently of equal merit — has made the joining of "different cultures" into "a single civic enterprise" improbable if not quite unlikely.

II.

In 1998 historian Jack Granatstein published a small book, *Who Killed Canadian History?* It quickly became a bestseller as it touched the raw nerves of an increasing number of Canadians, particularly in English-Canada, who had turned wary about the direction in which the country was headed. Three decades after Canadians came together to celebrate their country's centenary too much of divisive politics had pushed Canada to the brink of breaking down. It appeared the glue binding territorially a vast country and people with immensely diverse origins as immigrants was no longer holding, the core values which heralded the Canadian adventure had diminished over time and there, as always at such times, loomed the peril as the Irish poet W.B. Yeats once noted, "Things fall apart" when "the centre cannot hold."

Granatstein surveyed the state of knowledge about Canada's history among Canadians in general and, more specifically, among the young attending schools and colleges. A number of academics had done the same, and their findings revealed a poverty of knowledge among Canadians of their country's history that eventually caught the attention of politicians who scrambled, as did the Liberal government of Prime Minister Jean Chretien in 1997, to fund scholarships for students with incentives to study their country's past (Granatstein: chapter 6). This was a small step forward in the noble mission of paying attention to nation-building by fostering historical awareness among citizens of their country, and of acknowledging what should be obvious. "History," Granatstein wrote, "is no panacea for our national ailments. But a nation cannot forget its past, obliterate it, subdivide it into micro-histories, alter it, and bury it" (ibid: 148).

In identifying the causes that contributed to the general decline in historical awareness among the general public, Granatstein pointed to the spread of "multicultural mania" in the country since the passage of Trudeau's Multicultural Policy in 1971. This policy, it should be recalled, was adopted and promoted to assist immigrants to fully participate in the broader Canadian society. In a very short time this policy also became an instrument for giving immigrants resources to build their own self-images through what has come to be known as multicultural education, and to encourage the diverse ethnic communities to study the history of their own groups as distinct and apart from that of the country they have made home. The argument favouring multiculturalism is the need to recognize the many strands of history, or many histories, present in an ethnically diverse country. This is all to the good in the best liberal sense of learning about the human experience in history and when such learning is not made into a zero-sum game. But "multicultural mania" advanced the study of immigrant histories with political agenda attached in an ethnically diverse country at the expense of shared national history. Since Canada is predominantly "white" in racial term, the politics of multiculturally driven histories meant very quickly "the history of Canada, where it is even taught, has been distorted out of all recognition. Guilt, victimhood, redress, and the avoidance of offence — those are the watchwords that rule today" (Granatstein: 83). In other words the ascendancy of "political correctness" that frowns upon and is intolerant of anything spoken or written questioning, contradicting or violating multicultural sensibility, and that rules out in advance any critical discourse about "minority" cultural groups in a white majority society as discriminatory is greatly responsible for "killing Canadian history."

Multicultural education turned out to be the "politically correct" effort to counter the largely "white" dominant narrative of

West's history — Canada's history being part of this narrative — by increasing the focus on the histories of "non-white" people. Once again, the best of liberal education would require for the genuine advancement of our commonly shared knowledge of world history the broadening of the narrative to include the place, role and contributions of non-white people. But the unintended effect of multicultural education was the extent to which it was deliberately pushed to inflame "history wars" and make claims for identity politics. One of the most conspicuous examples, for instance, of "history wars" and identity politics was the work of Edward Said, the Palestinian-American Professor of English and Comparative Literature at New York's Columbia University. In his much discussed 1978 book *Orientalism*, Said advanced the argument that the study in the West of the Orient (primarily the Middle East, as it was his main concern) was driven by the necessity of power and strategic interests of European imperialist states, Britain and France, and later the United States. Said contended that the history of the Middle East was rendered by Western scholars in an essentialist manner by dehumanizing Arabs and Muslims, and representing them as the "other" of the civilized Europeans (Mansur: 69). Said wrote, "On the one hand there are Westerners, and on the other there are Arab-Orientals; the former are (in no particular order) rational, peaceful, liberal, logical, capable of holding real values, without natural suspicion; the latter are none of these things" (Said: 49). The study of the Orient and its depiction by Western scholars amounted to, according to Said, a "Western style for dominating, restructuring, and having authority over the Orient" (ibid: 3). He concluded, "It is therefore correct that every European, in what he could say about the Orient, was consequently a racist, an imperialist, and almost totally ethnocentric" (ibid: 204).

Said's work was an example of the sort of historical "deconstruction" for pushing the agenda of identity politics and multicultural education in the West. In accusing Western scholarship of reductionism in the study of the Middle East, Said engaged in reverse reductionism by explaining to Arabs and Muslims how the tremendously diverse West and its scholars are "racist" and "ethnocentric". Moreover, Said's work exemplified the negative aspect of what passed for scholarship in advancing claims on behalf of ethnic communities as part of the politics of multiculturalism. The most systematic repudiation of Said's shoddy work in "history wars" is that of Ibn Warraq (the pseudonym of a South Asian-American writer) in *Defending the West*. One reviewer of Ibn Warraq's critique of Said's writings wrote:

Said's incoherent amalgam of dubious postmodern theory, sentimental Third Worldism, glaring historical errors, and Western guilt corrupted not just Middle Eastern Studies departments, but other disciplines, too, such as English and "culture studies"... Most important is the observation that Said's relentless depiction of the "Orient" as a passive victim of the West — lacking its own agency, voice, or motivating values — ultimately paints a picture of Oriental inferiority even more distorted than his depictions of Western scholarship.[9]

Ibn Warraq showed how Said, consumed by his ideological pre-disposition, failed to recognize "the defining values of the Occident, or what are the tutelary guiding lights of, or the three golden threads running through, Western civilization — namely, rationalism, universalism, and self-criticism" (2007: 57). In their preoccupation with identity politics multiculturalists ignorantly or deliberately engage in unraveling these three golden threads woven into the fabric of the Western culture that have proven to be its strength, vibrancy and creativity in the making of the modern liberal democratic West.

The effect of multiculturalism has meant undermining through "history wars" the cultural integrity of Western countries or, as Arthur Schlesinger wrote, the "disuniting of America." The American vision, he observed in *The Disuniting of America: Reflections on a Multicultural Society*, "was not to preserve old cultures, but to produce a new *American* culture" (1998: 17). However, multiculturalism, he continued, as "the new ethnic gospel rejects the unifying vision of individuals from all nations melted into a new race. Its underlying philosophy is that America is not a nation of individuals at all but a nation of groups, that ethnicity is the defining experience for Americans, that ethnic ties are permanent and indelible, and that division into ethnic communities establishes the basic structure of American society and the basic meaning of American history" (ibid: 20-21). The same may be said of Canada or, differently stated,

---

[9] B.S. Thornton, "Golden Threads: Former Muslim Ibn Warraq stands up for the West," *City Journal*, August 17, 2007; available online www.city-journal.org.

Schlesinger feared the United States was becoming more like her northern neighbour.

III.

The example of Said's work illustrates how the characteristics of the open society are supportive of "history wars," which paradoxically then work in undermining that very openness. Since multiculturalism encouraged immigrants arriving in Canada to maintain their particular ethno-cultural identity, it meant immigrants importing into their newly adopted country the good, the bad and the ugly of their respective histories. This is what has happened. The conflicts, grievances and resentments from old countries found new soil to flourish. If multiculturalism was a policy to provide some intellectual heft to the old Canadian dilemma of being distinct as a country from the United States with its "melting pot" version of American identity, it also became a tool for immigrants to advance the politics of "separate and equal" as they were encouraged to maintain their own cultural identities without the burden being placed on them for assimilation into the Canadian national identity.

But, as Granatstein wrote, Canada "lacked a unifying nationalist myth that bound the country together." Moreover, "the colonial link to Britain meant that British monarchs and governors general, not Canadian leaders, sat at the top of the greasy pole. North American life absorbed those who came here, to be sure, but the psychic unifying force of North Americanism was substantially weaker in its Canadian variant" (Granatstein: 88). A weak nationalist identity was made even weaker by multiculturalism, and the compensating expectation that ethnic diversity would enrich the existing Anglo-French Canadian culture came spiced with quarrels of the old world and some of these were lethal.

In the early morning hour (around 0700 GMT) of June 23, 1985, an Air India Boeing 747 on transit from Toronto via Montreal enroute to New Delhi and Mumbai as Flight 182 exploded off the shore of Ireland. The hidden bomb planted by Sikh terrorists detonated at 31,000 feet and tore the plane apart with 329 passengers and crew on board killing all. Most of the passengers were Canadian citizens of Indian origin, and among them a majority consisted of women and children going for a summer vacation to visit their ancestral home in India. This was the single worst terrorist event in aviation history before Islamist terrorists carried out their suicide missions in the attacks on New York and Washington on September 11, 2001. The Air India bombing was hatched, prepared and executed by militant Canadian Sikhs in their openly declared support for their Sikh brethren waging a separatist war in Punjab, India. The pro-Khalistan Sikhs (*Khalistan* being the name for the desired independent Sikh state) exported their quarrels abroad, and in Canada Sikh militants found safe haven to engage in politics that ravaged India for more than a decade in the 1970s and 1980s. The turmoil in Punjab as Sikh secessionists escalated their struggle reverberated in the Indo-Canadian community, and the Air India bombing was linked to the Indian military's assault in June 1984 on the Golden Temple in Amritsar, Punjab, the holiest site of Sikhism, to flush out Sikh militants, the murder of Indian Prime Minister Indira Gandhi by her Sikh bodyguards on October 31, 1984, and the revenge killing of Sikhs in Delhi and elsewhere in India by Hindu supporters of the slain leader.

The Canadian investigation into the Air India bombing, the arrest of suspected Sikh militants, the assembling of the case for the crown prosecution, the eventual trial and then the acquittal of the two prime suspects — Ajaib Singh Bagri and Ripudaman Singh Malik — in the case stretched over nearly two decades. The acquittal of suspects on the basis of reasonable doubt meant as Kim Bolan, who doggedly devoted her professional career in journalism to reporting on the subject, concluded, "Ultimately, that loss of faith is the real legacy of the Air-India bombing. Canada failed to protect the innocent, to punish the guilty, and to bring out the truth" (2005: 365).

The terrible story of the Air India bombing in which Canadian citizens were murdered cannot be blamed on multiculturalism. It also cannot be denied, however, that multiculturalism provided the political environment in which the bloody conflict of a distant land, India, found the soil to flourish with deadly consequences. But this story of foreign quarrels imported into Canada by immigrants is not an isolated singular case. Other immigrants from other distant places have brought their quarrels and grievances along with their personal baggage into

Canada such as Tamils from Sri Lanka, Palestinians, Lebanese, Algerians and other Arabs from the Middle East, Somalis, Rwandans and others from Africa as in earlier years of Canadian history after 1867 Irish and Italian immigrants, for instance, brought with them their homegrown quarrels. Or the example of the Ukrainians who lived in large numbers in the old country within the Austro-Hungarian Empire that became enemy country in the First World War. "The senior Ukrainian bishop in Canada at the outbreak of war," wrote Granatstein, "urged his compatriots to be loyal to their emperor, Franz Joseph, an astonishingly ignorant and unthinking act that led to much hardship, especially for immigrants who had come to Canada for a new life in a country free of Old World hatred" (1998: 95). These quarrels have marked out invisible boundaries separating communities, and official multiculturalism in practice has meant, as in the story of Air India bombing, the state maintaining some distance as a neutral observer of activities within the immigrant communities even when such activities meant breaking of the country's laws.

The bitter after-taste of the Air India bombing was summarized by Kim Bolan. Multiculturalism where it should have counted most, providing the government and its agencies with a better understanding of the Canadian ethnic mosaic to prevent terrorism that took 329 lives of people on board Air India, failed. Could it be, Bolan asked, Canadians in general underplayed the significance of this crime because it "primarily affected people who weren't perceived to be our own — brown people with accents who we didn't accept as Canadians? But they are our own. Our own victims. Our own terrorists" (2005: 2).

IV.

"History wars" eventually confirm that history is paradoxical. Our quest to understand history is driven in part to explain conflicts and confusions in our midst, and to find answers that are both rationally and emotionally satisfactory. But despite our best efforts we fall short. It is because we are ourselves merely fragments of a totality beyond our reach, and all we can grasp at any time is a small part of that whole. Nicola Chiaromonte, a political philosopher, in *The Paradox of History* expressed this dilemma as follows, "Man is part of an infinitely changing and infinitely elusive whole, and the part can never understand or control the whole" (1985: 36).

Since identity of a people or an individual is shaped by the forces of history, the flux of identity or identity crisis that has come to occupy many thinkers on the subject reflects the speed with which vast changes globally in our time account for this crisis. The emergence of nation-states in Europe in the eighteenth and nineteenth centuries wrenched the identity of people from their previous attachments to a universal church or an empire and shaped the new nationalist identity provided by the territorially bounded state resting on the claims of self-determination by a people insisting on their belonging to a civic, ethno-lingual or cultural group. The nationalist identity became for a long time the most stable basis of attachment for a people to the state in which they lived. But this nationalist identity in a world of market forces that operate globally has come under immense pressures, and the fear or concern over old identities synonymous with nationalist identities tearing apart and over-run by attachments to even older identities of pre-modern past surfaced in the final two decades of the last century. Global market forces de-stabilized such apparently stalwart states as the former Soviet Union, a military superpower, and older more primitive identities of tribe and religion worked for its disintegration. Similarly, former Yugoslavia was wrenched apart by market forces, and tribal attachments re-surfaced in the Balkans with a vengeance. In a perceptive book *Jihad Vs. McWorld: How Globalism and Tribalism are Reshaping the World*, Benjamin Barber discussed at length the unforeseen consequences of this paradoxical development in contemporary history. Barber took the term *jihad* to describe the emergence of tribalism in the late 20th century. By jihad, he meant, in its mildest form "religious struggle on behalf of faith, a kind of Islamic zeal. In its strongest political manifestation, it means bloody holy war on behalf of partisan identity that is metaphysically defined and fanatically defended" (1996: 9). The pro-Khalistan Sikhs supported the jihad of their Sikh brethren in India, an armed struggle on behalf of a faith, Sikhism, with the aim to establish a Sikh state, Khalistan, in Punjab against India's secular democracy, and the bombing of Air India flight was part of this Sikh jihad.

The problem that Barber discussed, and what it means in terms of identity politics, brought one of America's most distinguished political scientists at Harvard, Samuel Huntington, to devote an entire book to how even the United States, the world's oldest republic, was affected by globalism and tribalism. Unlike Canada, the United States possesses core values taught and shared by a large majority of its citizens. At an earlier point in history ethnicity and race had played their parts in forging American identity, but with civil war and the emancipation of black slaves, open immigration and civil rights movement America moved beyond ethnicity and race. As America evolved, Huntington postulated, the vast country with an increasingly multiethnic population was held together with the core values asserted by her founding fathers, and he described them together as the "American Creed." This Creed, according to Huntington, was an expression of several key elements in American history:

The English language, Christianity; religious commitment, English concepts of the rule of law, the responsibility of rulers, and the rights of individuals; and dissenting Protestant values of individualism, the work ethic, and the belief that humans have the ability and the duty to try to create a heaven on earth, "a city on a hill." Historically, millions of immigrants were attracted to America because of this culture and the economic opportunities it helped to make possible (2004: xvi).

But America herself was under assault by the divisive interplay of identity politics. Huntington asked "Who are we? Where do we belong?" These questions are not limited to America only, they are unhinging old democracies and new states around the world. "The more general causes," Huntington wrote, "of these quests and questionings include the emergence of a global economy, tremendous improvements in communication and transportation, rising levels of migration, the global expansion of democracy, and the end both of the Cold War and of Soviet communism as a viable economic and political system" (ibid: 13). Huntington was more or less reflecting on how the "Barber effect" of tension between globalism and tribalism could also undermine America.

If the United States as a republican order can be shaken by the interplay of market forces, tribalism and political democracy, the situation of Canada under these circumstances is even more perilous. Barber writes:

Jihad pursues a bloody politics of identity. McWorld a bloodless economics of profit. Belonging by default to McWorld, everyone is a consumer; seeking a repository for identity, everyone belongs to some tribe. But no one is a citizen. Without citizens, how can there be democracy? (1996: 8)

And so we come full circle, driven by the paradoxes which are embedded in history, to one of the oldest political questions reaching back to the age of Aristotle: How can free individuals coming together to build a political community that is democracy in which their political identity is provided by citizenship of that community or state, continue to prosper under the stress of the "Barber effect"? Identity politics tends to divisiveness in democracy, while multiculturalism in pushing identity politics within a democracy gives aid to jihad. In the context of jihad the idea of citizenship is undermined and, consequently, democracy increasingly might well come to represent a market where people gather merely as consumers and seekers of profit with no abiding core set of values binding them together as free people and citizens. Such a situation over time would lead to the unraveling of a liberal democracy, such as Canada, and the ultimate melt down of its own historically evolved identity.

Chapter Five

FORBIDDING OF SPEECH AND THOUGHT

Freedom of expression is the foundation of human rights,
the source of humanity, and the mother of truth. To strangle
freedom of speech is to trample on human rights, stifle
humanity, and suppress truth.

– Liu Xiaobo, Nobel Prize for Peace 2010

Among the members of the European Union, the Netherlands came to be seen as a model of the post-modern multicultural state by the end of the last century. The terrible nightmarish experiences of the Second World War among the Dutch had receded, and the guilt over what happened to the Jews of Holland and those who sought refuge there from the Nazis in Germany, as did the family of Anne Frank once Hitler came to power in 1933, taught a new generation in the Netherlands to devote much effort in the making of an inclusive and tolerant society. This goal got quickly advanced without any serious opposition since the Netherlands is also that part of Europe where seeds of the Enlightenment took root early, where Jews found shelter in escaping from the Inquisition in Spain and Portugal in the sixteenth century as did the Protestant Huguenots fleeing from the religious strife in France in the seventeenth century. This is also where the embrace of liberalism during its formative period when John Locke sought refuge there in 1683 and found among the Dutch a favourable environment to do some of his important writings, including the *Letter on Toleration*, contributed to buttressing the country as a major commercial power with rapidly developing overseas colonies.

For all practical purposes the Netherlands had become in the half-century since the end of the war in 1945 one of Europe's most liberal democratic societies, and freedom here for the Dutch represented a corner of the world where people could live as they chose in a society proud of being open and permissive. Amsterdam, the Dutch capital, became the billboard of this permissive society where openness meant celebration of the gay culture of homosexuals, gender equality, tolerance of recreational drug, pornography, euthanasia and multiculturalism as post-war immigration gradually added colour to the population. In the midst of the quiet and deserving satisfaction among the Dutch in the success of building their version of open society there lurked, however, a dark side that few publicly wanted to discuss and yet many at a minimum began to grow wary about. This dark side burst into the open with two murders in Amsterdam, that of Pim Fortuyn in May 2002 and of Theo van Gogh in November 2004; and freedom in the most basic sense of all freedoms — freedom of speech — came to be held hostage by Amsterdam's Court of Appeals when it brought Geert Wilders, an elected member of the Dutch parliament to trial in January 2010 for speech that allegedly incited hatred and discrimination against Muslims and Islam.

Ian Buruma's *Murder in Amsterdam* is an insightful and sensitive account of the circumstances in his native country that led to the tragic deaths of Pim Fortuyn, a populist intellectual-turned politician, and Theo van Gogh, a film director-producer and journalist who thrived on controversy. Their deaths came about as a result of the unintended consequences of politics emanating from the turmoil of the Middle East and the wider world of Islam that stoked the rise of Islamism, or political Islam, and washed ashore in Europe infecting a segment of immigrant Muslim population. Immigrants and immigration bring stress in their wake to the native population, and even as open, tolerant and accommodating a society as that of the Dutch could not be insulated entirely from it. There were problems earlier, as Buruma writes, with immigrants, particularly the Moluccans from the former Dutch colony of Indonesia that were forgotten. But among new immigrants from Africa and the Middle East many were Muslims, and as the number of Muslims increased in the Netherlands as they did elsewhere in Europe Islam as a faith tradition and a culture began to pose a challenge of the sort that few Europeans had given much thought to or anticipated.

The arrival of immigrants of Muslim faith in Europe from her former colonies in the period following the end of colonialism in Asia and Africa did not pose at first any special problem. Britain, France and the Netherlands had ruled over colonies with substantial or even majority Muslim populations. These immigrants found work that Europeans were unwilling to do, and they contributed their share in the re-building of modern post-war Europe. But among the second and third-generation of the children of immigrants born in Europe were those who came to question the political arrangement and their place in it at the margins of European societies their parents, perhaps meekly, had accepted. They did not want to assimilate themselves by diluting their inherited culture into the society where they were born and educated. They asserted increasingly their identity in terms of the faith of their ancestors, and wanted equal treatment among others of their culture defined in terms of religion and its norms as traditionally practiced in lands which their parents left behind.

The politics of multiculturalism — the insistence by its proponents that all cultures being equal deserve equal respect and treatment — held out for the generation born in Europe of immigrant parents from former colonies the promise of inclusion into the majority European culture without any discrimination. But this promise could only be realized with difficulty if all parties affirming their respective identities were prepared to accommodate *equally* each other and respect the cultural values of each group in the bargain; and this would require, in other words, people of minority cultures — Muslims, Hindus, Sikhs and others — respecting the individualist-oriented secular values of liberal democracy in the same measure as they sought recognition of their values and respect for their religious-based identity. In practice, however, the majority European culture did most of the accommodating consistent with the working premise of multiculturalism, and the people of minority cultures did most of the demanding for equal respect of their cultural norms. The ground as a result was prepared for the sort of trouble that surfaced in the Netherlands with the two murders, and the indictment of Geert Wilders on charges of engaging in speech inciting hatred against Muslims as people of an identifiable minority culture.

In Britain the "Rushdie affair" foretold the problem to be expected. The publication of Salman Rushdie's novel *The Satanic Verses* in September 1988 was followed by Muslim demands for a ban on sales of the book and its withdrawal by the publisher. When such demands went unfulfilled protests grew, and on January 14, 1989 the novel was burned in a public demonstration by Muslims gathered in the city of Bradford, England. A month later on February 14 came the pronouncement of death sentence for the author by the Iranian religious leader Ayatollah Khomeini, and Rushdie with his wife was forced into hiding. Shabbir Akhtar, a Muslim activist of Pakistani-origin who caught public attention during this period while working as a community relations officer in Bradford, observed:

Salman Rushdie's *The Satanic Verses* is seen by Muslims as a calculated attempt to vilify and slander the Prophet of Islam. Not only has Rushdie said what he pleased about God, he has also taken liberties with Muhammad (1989: 1).

The early signs of the "clash of civilizations" in the making were visible in the tableau of the book burning scene from Bradford. The Bradford crowd venting their anger also exposed the contradictions at the core of multiculturalism, the demand in this instance by Muslims in Britain that the majority culture respect their sense of hurt and outrage by banning a book and, thereby, establish the precedent that free speech is not entirely free in a liberal democracy. This point was driven home by Shabbir Akhtar on behalf of Muslims in Britain and beyond. Akhtar wrote:

By early May 1989 two simple claims had been established beyond reasonable dispute: firstly, that Muslims of many shades of opinion had been genuinely and deeply offended by the contents of *The Satanic Verses* and, secondly, that freedom of speech was not absolute even in a liberal democratic society. But the issue was by no means resolved. While even liberal writers were happy to concede that some of Rushdie's allusions to the Koran were clearly blasphemous (in Muslim eyes), they did not interpret this to be *a* ground (let alone a *decisive* ground) for recommending a state ban. Both the deadlock and the apparent disagreement of principle behind it still remain and may indeed remain forever with us (ibid: 53; italics given).

The disagreement Shabbir Akhtar referred to turned bloody some years later in the streets of Amsterdam when Mohammed Bouyeri, a twenty-six year old Dutch citizen of Moroccan origin, took his outrage over the film-documentary *Submission*, which he considered to be an insult to Islam, and killed its producer-director Theo van Gogh in public. Bouyeri then pinned a note with a knife to the slain body addressed to Ayaan Hirsi Ali, the friend of van Gogh, that she would meet the same fate. For Bouyeri the crime of Hirsi Ali, not unlike Rushdie's, was defaming Islam and Muslims by words and in writing.

Hirsi Ali of Somali origin had arrived in Holland fleeing from the circumstances of a marriage arranged by her father to a man she did not know, and the subordinate status of a woman in a male-dominated Muslim society such as that of Somalia. By dint of hard work and courage she worked her way upwards in the Dutch society to eventually become an elected member in the parliament of her adopted country. But in the process Hirsi Ali discarded her belief in Islam, embraced the liberal and secular culture of the West, and subjected the faith of her ancestors to harsh criticism especially regarding the treatment of women. Hirsi Ali spoke and wrote from experience and, as a victim of the practice of female circumcision (or genital mutilation) in parts of Africa, her criticism carried the sort of credibility born of personal injury that Muslim apologists and defenders of multiculturalism were in no position to rebut. She prepared the script for *Submission* selecting verses from the Quran to be displayed on the bodies of several partially clad women in various stages of ritual prayers indicating the servile status of women in Islamic culture, and Theo van Gogh turned the script into film. Hirsi Ali was driven into hiding, and as the political controversy and public unrest grew in Holland over van Gogh's killing Hirsi Ali retired from politics. But this was not enough. Hirsi Ali was required to leave her well-guarded residential building in The Hague when her immigration status in the Netherlands was questioned by her once political allies, forcing her to depart for the United States. In the postscript at the end of his book, *Murder in Amsterdam*, Ian Buruma lamented, "Theo van Gogh is dead. Mohammed Bouyeri is locked up in prison alone with the words of his holy books. And Ayaan Hirsi Ali has had to leave the scene. My country seems smaller without her."

90

II.

The "Rushdie affair" became the template of the campaign, pushed by Muslims and their innumerable organizations in the West, to restrict free speech in Europe and North America on the grounds that free speech cannot be a license to offend the feelings of cultural and religious minorities. Salman Rushdie did not commit any crime, nor had he broken any British or European law in the writing of his fictions including the novel *The Satanic Verses*. He was known to be a man of the left, an opponent of Prime Minister Margaret Thatcher's Conservative government in Britain, and a defender of immigrants in their effort to gain equal treatment in their adopted country. But none of that mattered to those Muslims, a majority in Britain from South Asia, who saw Rushdie's fiction as a thinly disguised insult directed at their faith and their prophet. Their outrage was heard back in India, Pakistan and Bangladesh. In October 1988 the Indian government under instructions of Prime Minister Rajiv Gandhi placed Rushdie's novel on the list of proscribed books fearing communal disturbances ahead of the scheduled federal election for the following year. Malise Ruthven writing about the "Rushdie affair" astutely observed, "In the electronic age, the quarrels of frontier villages erupt into people's living rooms every day" (1990: 163).

Salman Rushdie was, ironically saved by the *fatwa* (an Islamic religious ruling) of Ayatollah Khomeini calling for his death that sent him into hiding, or he might have met the fate of Theo van Gogh in the hands of some enraged Muslim. There could not have been a more clear and unambiguous indication than what was provided by the "Rushdie affair" that freedom of speech, as one of the fundamental principles of liberal democracy, was under assault. But neither the governments nor the public in the West were seriously alarmed by the notion that in the late twentieth century anyone needed to worry about demands to ban books, put limits on free speech, censor films, forbid making cartoons of certain subjects, and be fearful for the safety of public individuals should they speak and write on Islam and related matters that offend Muslims. Yet this is the direction in which the West was headed with the "Rushdie affair" even as the Berlin Wall got dismantled, a divided Europe became re-united, and the Soviet Union disintegrated.

The murders in Amsterdam in the aftermath of the terrorist attacks on New York City and Washington on September 11, 2001, and with Hirsi Ali requiring protection as was extended by the British government to Salman Rushdie, indicated the extent to which freedom of speech came under siege across the West. In such circumstance the irreverent cartoon drawings of Muhammad, the prophet of Islam, published in the Danish newspaper *Jyllands-Posten* on September 20, 2005 amounted to throwing a lighted fire into a tanker full of oil. These cartoons enraged Muslim opinion and violence erupted across the Middle East and beyond directed at the Danish embassies with demands for apology, retraction of the cartoons, punishment for the cartoonists, and boycott of Danish goods. The controversy unfolded as a repeat of the "Rushdie affair" in a much more hostile environment of the post-9/11 world. And, if I may quote from my writing about the events, "Muslim outrage was part spontaneous and part organized, and in varying measures seized upon by religious leaders, dictators, political opportunists, demagogues and rascals of all stripes, turned into a witch's brew and released into public space to go rampaging as demonstration of Muslim rage against those who profane what Muslims revere as sacred" (Mansur: 60).

The controversy over the Danish cartoons removed the veil for all to see how fragile is freedom of speech and how easily it can be undermined when its custodians are unwilling to defend it. As an act of solidarity with the besieged Danish newspaper *Jyllands-Posten*, and its editor Fleming Rose, a number of European newspapers and magazines in Italy, Germany, France, Spain and elsewhere published those same cartoons for their readers. But there were as many media outlets, both print and broadcasting, in Europe and North America that decided against publishing the cartoons as an act of self-censorship. This self-censorship meant, as Bruce Bawer in *Surrender: Appeasing Islam, Sacrificing Freedom* discussed, the custodians of freedom in the West were abandoning their posts out of fear of Muslim penchant for violence in countering real or perceived denigration of their belief. Bawer wrote:

Not all the major news media in Europe followed the example of *Le Monde* and *Die Welt*. No British newspaper ran the cartoons. Britain's Channel Four, Peter Whittle noted, "debated whether or not freedom of expression was threatened, concluded it was not, and then with spectacular absurdity refrained from showing the cartoons for fear of causing offense." Nor did *Jyllands-Posten* receive much support from its fellow news media in Scandinavia. American editors, too, proved, cowardly. Only one major daily in the United States — the *Philadelphia Inquirer* — reprinted any of the cartoons. Seattle's alternate weekly, *The Stranger*, published the most famous of the cartoons — the one by *Jyllands-Posten* staff cartoonist Kurt Westergaard showing Muhammad with a bomb in his turban — to illustrate a piece by me about the cartoons. But while *The Stranger*'s editors had the guts to do this — as did innumerable bloggers — the mighty broadcast networks CBS, NBC, ABC, and Fox did not. Nor did the cable news channel CNN, MSNBC, and Fox News. In an editorial, the *New York Times* defended its refusal to print the cartoons as "a reasonable choice for news organizations that usually refrain from gratuitous assaults on religious symbols." (Describing this editorial as "a characteristically pompous and ponderous piece of chin-stroking sanctimony," Gerard Baker of the *Times* of London dryly recalled that the Gray Lady had in the past run pictures of "works of art such as a crucifix in a vat of urine or an icon of the Virgin Mary covered in elephant dung.") The magazine *Free Inquiry* reprinted the cartoons — but both the Borders Books and Waldenbooks chains refused to sell the issue in question. In all of Canada, only two marginal publications, the *Western Standard* and *Jewish Free Press*, reprinted them; both were reported to the Alberta Human Rights Commission (2009: 46).

This refusal by the mainstream politicians and the mainstream media to vigorously defend freedom of speech was predictably explained in terms of prudential restraint to avoid provoking domestic unrest. Both George W. Bush in the White House at the time when the Danish cartoon controversy erupted and former president Bill Clinton expressed their dismay with the cartoons as did a number of prominent intellectuals (ibid). Roger Scruton, the conservative English philosopher, opined that while freedom of speech is "one of the bastions of democratic government, and it has been clear at least since John Stuart Mill's eloquent defence of it that, without free speech, we are likely to be locked into mistaken policies until the point comes when we can no longer correct them", yet "we ought also to recognize that freedom of speech does not mean the freedom to produce images, however offensive, or to make insulting gestures."[10] Again, such

---

[10] R. Scruton, "Respect, and a real debate," in *Muslims and Europe: a cartoon confrontation*, openDemocracy, February 6, 2006; available online (www.opendemocracy.net).

reactions were not dissimilar to what was said by many prominent public figures when Salman Rushdie was forced into hiding.

When the "Rushdie affair" broke out former president Jimmy Carter went public stating, "Rushdie's book is a direct insult to those millions of Muslims whose sacred beliefs have been violated... The death sentence proclaimed by Ayatollah Khomeini, however, was an abhorrent response. It is our duty to condemn the threat of murder [but] we should be sensitive to the concern and anger that prevails even among more moderate Muslims."[11] Sir Geoffrey Howe, the British foreign secretary at the time, speaking as much for himself as likely for many of his colleagues, said, "The British government, the British people, do not have any affection for the book... It compares Britain with Hitler's Germany. We do not like that any more than the people of the Muslim faith like the attacks on their faith contained in the book. So we are not sponsoring the book. What we are sponsoring is the right of people to speak freely, to publish freely" (ibid). The highly regarded writer of spy thrillers John LeCarre declared, "Again and again, it has been within his [Rushdie's] power to save the faces of his publisher and, with dignity, withdraw his book until a calmer time has come... It seems to me he has nothing more to prove except his own insensitivity" (ibid.). And author Roald Dahl noted that Rushdie "knew exactly what he was doing and cannot plead otherwise. This kind of sensationalism does indeed get an indifferent book on to the top of the bestseller list — but to my mind it is a cheap way of doing it" (ibid). The response of the Western governments and leaders were at best confused. The government of Prime Minister Brian Mulroney in Ottawa issued a temporary ban on importing *The Satanic Verses*; there was silence initially from Prime Minister Margaret Thatcher and the opposition leader Neil Kinnock in London, and none among the Muslims calling for the killing of Rushdie was charged with incitement to murder which is a punishable offense in Britain; in Washington President George H.W. Bush thought both the book and the call for the murder of the author by the Iranian leader were repugnant; the strongest response from a European leader was that of France's President François Mitterrand condemning the death threat against Rushdie as "absolute evil" (Pipes: 155-159). But the *New York*

---

[11] Cited in A. Anthony, "How one book ignited a culture war," *The Observer*, January 11, 2009; available online (www.guardian.co.uk).

Times, unlike the stand it took over the Danish cartoons, published an editorial that declared:

Islam deserves to be treated with respect and its horror of blasphemy needs to be understood. Jimmy Carter and New York's Cardinal O'Connor are right to plead for such understanding. But no amount of understanding can condone a call for murder. This barbarism needs to be denounced over and again until the threat is withdrawn.

Nor should striving to understand another's principles lead to surrendering one's own. Some Americans come close to suggesting that free speech is a complicated Western concept inapplicable to other societies. This is bad logic and worse policy. Should one by this logic remain mute if non-Western societies condone slavery, torture, infanticide and the immolation of widows?

Free speech is a universal good, not a Western idiosyncrasy. It grew out of the struggle for religious toleration, and opens the way to peaceful coexistence of all faiths. The wise remedy whenever someone feels wronged by someone else's free speech is more free speech. To excuse book-burnings, whether in England or India, is to throw reason itself on the pyre.

Free speech is not a self-executing principle. It demands continued defense, and especially when the circumstances are dangerous — or wearily familiar. Whether Salman Rushdie is a blasphemer or preacher, a pedant or a poet, he is entitled to the world's unwavering support.[12]

This editorial was admirable and robust in defending a besieged author under death threat, and the principle of freedom of speech. Yet in less than twenty years the effects of multiculturalism worked their way through much of the Western world as they did through the editorial boardroom of the *Times*, and one such effect was that when it came to opposing the outlandish behaviour of people from "non-Western societies" during the Danish cartoon controversy the mainstream media went mostly mute.

The reluctance to defend free speech might also be explained by the self-imposed inhibition of the mainstream media, politicians and intellectuals fearing criticism of political incorrectness. For more than a generation people in the West were instructed in "political correctness," as a corollary of multiculturalism, which taught the public not to speak or write in a manner that could offend people in a

---

[12] *New York Times* editorial, "The Rushdie Affair Lives," April 16, 1989.

multicultural society. The requirement to be polite, decent, civil and considerate towards less fortunate or more vulnerable members of the society is commonsense and uncontentious. But when such a requirement is made into a doctrine, and when such doctrine requires a suspension of discourse that is critical or judgmental on the basis of *discriminating* among things, ideas, people and cultures then such a politically correct society is trading politeness and decency to become a society that is dogmatic and intolerant of dissenting opinions. In such a doctrinaire environment an individual accused of political incorrectness would be considered a bigot. This was the result of how political correctness took the word *discriminate* — meaning to distinguish between or among things — and turned it entirely negative to mean drawing differences on the basis of race, ethnicity and colour. Hence political correctness, irrespective of whatever good intentions there was at its beginning, became increasingly over time in practice inimical to liberalism that values individual right to dissent, to hold unorthodox opinions, to question or be skeptical of majority consensus, and to defend freedom of speech especially when any speech is considered offensive by some segment of the population. And contrary to the notion that multiculturalism is about diversity, a multicultural society shaped by political correctness increasingly insists upon conformity of opinion and throws a blanket of chill over free speech.

III.

Salman Rushdie survived the threat to his life by going into hiding arranged for him by the British government, and then moved on as a celebrated writer successfully publishing other works of fiction. But other lesser known figures, some associated with Rushdie's novel *The Satanic Verses*, were not as fortunate. Rushdie's Japanese translator Hitoshi Igarashi, a professor of literature and Middle Eastern studies at Tsukuba University in Japan, was stabbed to death on campus in July 1991. Rushdie's Italian translator Ettore Capriolo, and Norwegian translator William Nygaard, were both seriously wounded in knife attacks. The most serious incident of violence, however, took place in July 1993 in the town of Sivas, Turkey. A mob attacked the building where a cultural conference was in session. The mob had come looking for Aziz Nesin, the Turkish translator of *The Satanic Verses*, and in failing to capture him the mob set the building on fire and prevented firefighters from extinguishing the blaze that killed thirty-seven people. Nesin escaped, but he was blamed by the state attorney Nusrat Demiral for the provocation that resulted in mob violence and deaths. Farag Foda, liberal thinker and staunch critic of Muslim fundamentalists, was murdered in Cairo in June 1992; Naguib Mahfouz, the renowned Egyptian novelist and Nobel Prize winner, survived a knife attack in 1994 for his liberal views unacceptable to the same people who killed Foda. Taslima Nasreen, writer and free-thinking woman in Bangladesh, was accused by Muslim fundamentalists for apostasy for her critical views about religious laws in Islam and as a result forced into exile in 1994.

The list is long of those Muslims and ex-Muslims in speaking and writing critically of Islam and Muslim history who have had to flee their native country, risk being killed, or write under a pseudonym as the author of *Why I Am Not a Muslim* does under the pen name of Ibn Warraq. The case of Ayaan Hirsi Ali is a notable addition to this list; yet this list is of people who by their origin have known the perils of engaging in any criticism of their religion at the hands of fellow Muslims. Their situation indicates how alien is the idea and culture of free speech in contemporary Islam, of how unacceptable is the notion that Islam, as any other religion, might be critically examined. The case of Nasr Hamid Abu Zayd (1943-2010), professor of literature at the Cairo University, illustrated the peril for Muslims re-thinking Islam under the shadow of the "Rushdie affair" as Muhammad Iqbal, the poet-philosopher in undivided British India, had called for in his lectures given in 1930 published under the title *The Reconstruction of Religious Thought in Islam*. Nasr Hamid Abu Zayd applied the methods of hermeneutics to the study of the Qur'an, and this effort resulted in the charge of apostasy brought by Muslim fundamentalists against him. He was not sentenced to death by religious authorities or the government, but his marriage was dissolved on the religious grounds that a believing Muslim woman could not be married to a non-Muslim. Nasr Hamid Abu Zayd fled Egypt with his wife in 1995 to take refuge in Holland, as did Taslima Nasreen for a life in exile in Europe.

On freedom of speech the view of "official" Islam, as represented by the member-states and governments of the Organization of Islamic Conference, is set forth in the Cairo Declaration of August 1990. Article 22 (a) of the OIC statement reads, "Everyone shall have the right to express his opinion freely in such manner as would not be contrary to the principles of the Shari'ah." The requirement for Muslims, as set down by the Cairo Declaration, is resist engaging in any discussion of Islam that might be viewed as blasphemy bringing with it the charge of apostasy that is considered a capital crime. From this perspective an ex-Muslim is an apostate from Islam, and under *shari'ah* rule would face capital punishment. A contemporary scholar of Islamic laws explains, "In a culture whose lynchpin is religion, religious principles and religious morality, apostasy is in some way equivalent to high treason in the modern nation-state" (Hallaq: 319). The "Rushdie affair" shows Muslims, ex-Muslims, and even non-Muslims, can be subject to the charge of apostasy if authorities of "official" Islam believe they have committed blasphemy by insulting the prophet or criticizing Islam even when residing in countries outside the world of Islam as were Salman Rushdie and his translators.

But the "Rushdie affair" also raised the question why should a non-Muslim under any circumstance be liable for causing offense to Muslims by writing about Islam critically or unfavourably. Christopher Hitchens, a widely respected journalist and controversial author, raised this question observing, "Salman [Rushdie] was raised as a Muslim, so in theory he's within the jurisdiction. He can be sentenced as an apostate, and the same can be done to Ayaan Hirsi Ali and Taslima Nasreen. But what people haven't noticed sufficiently is that now people who are not Muslims, like the Danish cartoonists, have been threatened with violence for criticizing Islam. That's sort of new, and ought to be more controversial than it is."[13] The situation is worsened, however, when government agencies in the West indict individuals under hate-speech laws for offending Muslims. When this occurs, as with the trial of Geert Wilders in the Amsterdam's Court of Appeal, then Western governments are conceding space to "official" Islam and to Islamists in their midst by accommodating, in practical

---

[13] Anthony, *op.cit.*

terms, their demand for acceptance of *shari'ah* directives in secular and liberal society.

IV.

The trial of Geert Wilders, leader of the Netherlands' Freedom Party, in Amsterdam's Court of Appeals ostensibly was not about freedom of speech protected by article 7 of the Dutch constitution, and article 10 of the European Convention on Human Rights to which Holland is a signatory. The case against Wilders was about "inciting hatred" towards a recognizable group, Muslims in Holland, under articles 137c and 137d of the Dutch Penal Code. The evidence put together to indict Wilders was contained in a dossier of public statements, interviews, and newspaper articles about Islam and Muslims he had made, and the anti-Islam documentary film, *Fitna*, he produced. Folkert Jensma, a Dutch journalist following the case, reported:

[the] court found that freedom of political speech should lead to a socially acceptable contribution to public debate. This is not the case here. The criminal code therefore has a role to play if "the contribution to public debate is unnecessarily injurious to a group of believers in encroaching on their religious dignity, while that contribution simultaneously incites hatred, intolerance, enmity and discrimination". There are citizens, and politicians, "who have been sentenced on the ground of less far-reaching statements than Wilders", the court stated last year.[14]

It was unlikely that Wilders would get indicted for inciting hatred and discrimination against an identifiable minority group were it not for the troubled reality in Holland, and Europe, brought about by the explosive situation of the Islamist based "homegrown terror." In Wilders' case the complaint by the left-wing group, the Nederland Bekent Kleur (NBK, "Colourful Netherlands"), was initially dismissed by the public prosecutor's office doubtful whether any crime had been committed. But Wilders was eventually acquitted of all charges

---

[14] F. Jensma, "Has Wilders broken the law?" *Radio Netherlands Worldwide*, January 19, 2010.

against him by the Court of Appeals, and though this might not be the end of his legal troubles with left-wing opponents the court's decision rescued Holland's reputation as a free and open society.[15] In the court's view Wilders remarks on Islam and comparison made of the Qur'an to Hitler's *Mein Kampf*, though considered "rude and denigrating," were viewed as rhetoric at the edge of what is legally permissible without being illegal. The court ruling suggested such speech found offensive by some and not by others should be tested in the court of public opinion and not the court of law.

The lawyer, Ties Prakken, representing complainants against Geert Wilders responded to the Court of Appeal's decision by indicating that since legal avenues were exhausted in the Netherlands, she would prepare an appeal to the UN Commission on Human Rights in Geneva. The appeal could also be filed with the European Court at Strasbourg, and such an appeal would test the limits of article 10 of the European Convention on Human Rights. The recent rulings of the European Court suggest it favours measures to curb racism and incitements to racism within Europe. Article 10 places restrictions on free speech as prescribed by law and, in part the article reads, that such limits are "necessary in a democratic society, in the interests of national security, territorial integrity or public safety, for the prevention of disorder or crime, for the protection of health or morals, for the protection of the reputation or the rights of others". The complainants against Wilders sought to stifle by legal means any critical discussion relating to Islam, a minority religion in Europe, and which would then set the precedent for remarks viewed as hateful by Muslims, or similarly by any other religious group, could then be considered offensive and liable to prosecution.

There has not been another case like that of Geert Wilders, a sitting member of parliament, in a liberal democracy such as the Netherlands. But freedom of speech in general in the West is under siege, and the argument made in limiting free speech in support of multiculturalism is that the privileged status of free speech is unwarranted, and a single value should not trump all others in a multicultural society (Parekh: 320). In Canada the constraints on free speech have come about in recent years from the various human rights commissions, and the complaints brought against Ezra Levant and

---

[15] "Wilders not guilty on all charges," *DutchNews.nl*, June 23, 2011.

those against Mark Steyn and *Maclean's* illustrate the precarious state of freedom of speech in one of the world's oldest democracies.

Ezra Levant was the publisher of the *Western Standard*, a small centre-right magazine of news and opinion in Canada published in Calgary, Alberta. In the February 13, 2006 issue of the magazine Ezra Levant reproduced the Danish cartoons for his readers. A few days later Syed Soharwardy, a Canadian of Pakistani origin residing in Calgary, filed a complaint with the Alberta Human Rights and Citizenship Commission (AHRCC) against the magazine and its publisher for causing him offense as a Muslim by displaying the Danish cartoons. For the next two years the AHRCC embroiled Ezra Levant in defending the publication of these cartoons as a constitutionally guaranteed right of the freedom of expression, and as a newsworthy item in a newsmagazine. The *Western Standard* went out of publishing in print editions in October 2007, but the complaint launched by Syed Soharwardy proceeded until withdrawn by the complainant in 2008 when the controversy surrounding the case turned into a public relations problem for the AHRCC. Ezra Levant has written a gripping account of his experience in *Shakedown* that stands as a cautionary tale of how democracy is under assault in the name of human rights. When Soharwardy decided to withdraw his complaint he left behind for the taxpayers, as Ezra Levant writes:

[a] $500,000 tab for the AHRCC's investigation and me and the *Western Standard* with the better part of $100,000 in expenses. He just walked away, without a penny of penalties or even an apology. A few months later, with Soharwardy out of the picture, the AHRCC quietly snuffed out the piggyback complaint from the Edmonton Council of Muslim Communities. I'd won – even if it didn't feel like a victory (2009: 152).

The complaint against the *Western Standard* and Ezra Levant was followed by the complaint against the newsmagazine *Maclean's* filed in 2007 with human rights commissions in the provinces of British Columbia and Ontario, and with the Canadian Human Rights Commission in Ottawa, by Mohamed Elmasry of the Canadian Islamic Congress. Elmasry's complaint was similar to that of Syed Soharwardy's that *Maclean's*, in publishing in October 2006 an article by Mark Steyn under the heading "The future belongs to Islam", had infringed the rights of Muslims in Canada not to be discriminated against as a group.

Mark Steyn's article in *Maclean's* was an extended extract from his best-selling book *America Alone* published in the United States in 2006. In the book, and the extract *Maclean's* published, Mark Steyn discussed how the emerging demographic reality of Europe — an aging population declining as a result of negative fertility rate, growth in immigration from non-European countries of Asia and Africa, and the rising trend in numbers of Muslim immigrant population — might likely shape the politics and culture of the continent in the twenty-first century. Elmasry found the Mark Steyn piece discriminatory and offensive personally and as the head of an organization that claimed to represent Muslims in Canada. But Elmasry was himself tainted by controversy for the remarks made on television during a panel discussion on *The Michael Coren Show* in October 2004. Elmasry declared during an exchange on the subject of terrorism with the host, Michael Coren, that all adult Israelis, 18-year and older, were valid targets of attacks by Palestinian terrorists. For Elmasry, a professor in the engineering faculty of the University of Waterloo in Ontario, it was passing strange that he was offended by an article in one of English Canada's prestigious newsmagazine given his own public profile loaded with controversy following his remarks made to Coren, and which he would not withdraw when given an opportunity by the host on the show until he was forced to offer an unconditional public apology by the dean of his faculty.

Elmasry filed his complaint against *Maclean's* in three jurisdictions presumably expecting that at least one of the human rights commissions would rule in his favour. In the complaint filed with the Ontario Human Rights Commission (complaint number LHOR-72JP9D), Elmasry made a list of 46 items on reading Mark Steyn's piece that he viewed as defamatory and which he claimed caused him anguish. The effect or anguish caused by reading *Maclean's* was such, Elmasry concluded in his complaint, that it "included harm to my sense of dignity and self-worth as a Canadian Muslim." Elmasry was to be disappointed when the rulings from each of the three human rights commissions dismissed his complaint.

The complaints against the *Western Standard* and *Maclean's* brought to focus for the public subsection 13(1) of the Canadian Human Rights Act (CHRA), and similar articles provided in the respective human rights codes of British Columbia and Ontario. The CHRA was enacted as a statute in 1977, and its purpose was stated in article 2 as follows:

The purpose of this Act is to extend the laws in Canada to give effect, within the purview of matters coming within the legislative authority of Parliament, to the principle that all individuals should have an opportunity equal with other individuals to make for themselves the lives that they are able and wish to have and to have their needs accommodated, consistent with their duties and obligations as members of society, without being hindered in or prevented from doing so by discriminatory practices based on race, national or ethnic origin, colour, religion, age, sex, sexual orientation, marital status, family status, disability or conviction for an offence for which a pardon has been granted.

The creation of the federal human rights commission in Canada, followed by the provinces doing the same, was a "beautiful idea" in the words of Ezra Levant. It was established, as article 2 stated, to provide for an equitable and fair settlement of disputes outside of courts resulting from any sort of discrimination against an individual or group in society. The original statute included a section against "publication of discriminatory notices" and later section 13 was added against "hate messages." The provision of section 13 in the CHRA in addition to section 319 of the Criminal Code of Canada against public incitement liable to lead to breach of peace, placed limits on the freedom of expression otherwise guaranteed by the Canadian Charter of Rights and Freedoms. The purpose and scope of section 13 are as follows:

13. (1) It is a discriminatory practice for a person or a group of persons acting in concert to communicate telephonically or to cause to be so communicated, repeatedly, in whole or in part by means of the facilities of a telecommunication undertaking within the legislative authority of Parliament, any matter that is *likely* to expose a person or persons to hatred or contempt by reason of the fact that that person or those persons are identifiable on the basis of a prohibited ground of discrimination (*italics* added).

Interpretation

(2) For greater certainty, subsection (1) applies in respect of a matter that is communicated by means of a computer or a group of interconnected or related computers, including the Internet, or any similar means of communication, but does not apply in respect of a matter that is communicated in whole or in part by means of the facilities of a broadcasting undertaking.

The phrasing in subsection 13 (1) that any communication "likely" to cause offence by exposing an individual or group to hatred or discrimination leaves the definition of what constitutes hate speech to be open-ended, subjective and stacked in favour of complainants. The word "likely" is an invitation for charges to be brought against someone expressing *thought* that is viewed offensive, and that someone is then considered guilty within the framework of the CHRA until — contrary to the cherished principle of innocent until proven guilty — he establishes his innocence. This open-endedness, therefore, exposes anyone engaged in public discourse to the *likely* charge of hate-speech as it happened to Ezra Levant when Syed Soharwardy filed a complaint against him with the AHRCC.

Elmasry's complaint was based on section 13 of the CHRA. In dismissing the complaint the Canadian Human Rights Commission in Ottawa took note that the views expressed by Mark Steyn in the *Maclean's* article were not of extreme nature, and did not meet the minimal requirement of hate speech under subsection 13 (1) that would warrant appointment of a Tribunal to hear the evidence. But the public interest in and the subsequent affront with what was involved in Elmasry's complaint generated enough pressure in the media that the Commissioner of the CHRC, Jennifer Lynch, was driven to arrange a public inquiry into the problems of hate speech with special reference to section 13. Lynch appointed Richard Moon, professor of law at the University of Windsor, Ontario, to report back to the CHRC with recommendations after public hearings on the matter.

Ezra Levant, Mark Steyn and *Maclean's* were high profile defendants in hate speech complaints brought to the human rights commissions in Canada. Their cases caught the public's attention unlike those regularly brought against individuals without high profiles who willingly settled, fearing the costs of hearings and fines if found guilty, for some sums of money with complainants as adjudicated by the HRCs. Instead Ezra Levant, and *Maclean's* owned by the Canadian telecommunication giant Rogers Media, were prepared to fight any rulings against them by the HRCs in the courts. When the furor over the Danish cartoons broke and Ezra Levant was served notice by the AHRCC for publishing them in the *Western Standard* Alan Borovoy, general counsel of the Canadian Civil Liberties Association and one of the original proponents of human rights legislation, came out in public against what he saw as an infringement of free speech. Borovoy wrote:

Despite my considerable involvement in pressuring the Ontario government, many years ago, to create Canada's first human rights commission, I regret this use of the law. It's one thing to invoke the law against discriminatory deeds; it's another thing entirely to employ it against discriminatory words.

During the years when my colleagues and I were labouring to create such commissions, we never imagined that they might ultimately be used against freedom of speech.

There should be no question of the right to publish the impugned cartoons.

Religious prophets no less than political leaders or even deities must be legally permissible targets of satire or even scorn. This is the essence of free speech in a democracy.

No ideology — political, religious or philosophical — can be immune.

It would be best, therefore, to change the provisions of the Human Rights Act to remove any such ambiguities of interpretation.[16]

Borovoy was not alone in seeing the peril to free speech residing within the human rights legislation. Keith Martin, Liberal Member of Parliament in Ottawa for Esquimalt-Juan de Fuca in British Columbia, moved a private member's notice of motion on January 30, 2008 stating, "in the opinion of the House, subsection 13 (1) of the Canadian Human Rights Act should be deleted from the Act."

In October 2008 Richard Moon, acting as one-man commission of inquiry, presented his report to Jennifer Lynch. He wrote:

---

[16] A. Borovoy, "Hearing Complaint alters Rights Body's Mandate," *The Calgary Herald*, March 16, 2006.

The principal recommendation of this report is that section 13 be repealed so that the censorship of Internet hate speech is dealt with exclusively by the criminal law. A narrowly drawn ban on hate speech that focuses on expression that is tied to violence does not fit easily or simply into a human rights law that takes an expansive view of discrimination and seeks to advance the goal of social equality through education and conciliation...

The restriction of hate speech that threatens, advocates or justifies violence is appropriately dealt with under the criminal law. In the words of the Cohen Committee, "No civil statute can create a moral standard equivalent to that of criminal law." Hate speech is a serious matter that should be investigated by the police and prosecuted in the courts and should carry a significant penalty (2008: 31).

Moon's recommendation was heartening to defenders of free speech in Canada. Keith Martin came out in support of Moon, and reminding Canadians of his private member's motion in parliament wrote:

In the end, as Prof. Moon says in his report, we have Criminal Code amendments that thankfully protect all of us from hate crimes and hate speech. Thus, it is within the Criminal Code, not the CHRC, that hate crimes and hate speech should be prosecuted.

In an open and liberal democracy, we have a right to be protected from hate speech, but we do not have a right to not be offended. Canadians laid down their lives in two world wars to give us the cherished right of free speech. It is now the duty of Parliamentarians to stand up and protect it.[17]

But Keith Martin's motion did not bring the House of Commons to take any measure in defence of free speech by adopting Professor Moon's recommendation to repeal section 13 of the CHRA. Instead we find the hold of the human rights industry in Canada, as well as other democracies in the West, has far exceeded the initial purpose, erroneous though it was as Borovoy conceded, of protecting individuals from bigotry or being offended by placing limits on free speech. In the pursuit of eliminating real or perceived discrimination in an officially declared multicultural society, as is Canada, by prosecuting what might be deemed to be "hate" speech governments mistakenly legislated human rights codes that have put in jeopardy fundamental unalienable rights of individuals constitutionally

---

[17] K. Martin, "Revise the Human Rights Act," *National Post*, November 26, 2008.

recognized and protected in liberal democracies. Of what this means Karen Selick, a lawyer with the Canadian Constitution Foundation, has written,

Human rights codes have fabricated a phoney "right" to be free from discrimination and used it to override a panoply of genuine human rights, including: freedom of expression, freedom of association, freedom of contract and control over one's private property. There can be no such thing as the right to violate someone else's rights. It's a contradiction in terms. The only solution to this seeming paradox is the complete repeal of the human rights codes, not mere changes to the enforcement mechanisms.[18]

The reasoning on the part of politicians of all parties to resist the idea of repealing section 13 could be the reticence historically in Canada with uncensored free speech, and this has grown stronger with the embrace of multiculturalism and its corollary of political correctness intolerant of any speech objected to as "hate speech" by people of minority culture. In speaking to an American audience at the Plattsburg State University in Plattsburg, New York in April 2004 Canada's Chief Justice Beverley McLachlin dwelled upon the subject of free speech, and how Americans and Canadians view it differently in terms of their respective constitutions. Justice McLachlin explained:

[L]et us consider the constitutional protection of free speech in both countries. Canada, like the United States, has a constitutional guarantee of free expression. Our *Charter of Rights and Freedoms* guarantees freedom of expression, subject to such reasonable limits as are "demonstrably justifiable in a free and democratic society." In other words, we have free speech, but the state can limit it in reasonable ways. This may be contrasted with the absolute language of the First Amendment of the United States Bill of Rights, which states: "Congress shall make no law...abridging the freedom of speech or of the press." The words of the Canadian guarantee acknowledge the state's right to limit free speech; the words of the American guarantee forbid the state from doing so (2004).

In elaborating further on the differences, Justice McLachlin stated, "To put it in a nutshell, we in Canada are more tolerant of state

---

[18] K. Selick, "The real problem with human rights tribunals," *Ottawa Citizen*, May 20, 2011.

limitation on free expression than are Americans" (ibid). The reason for the differences is that the Canadian "approach to the constitutional protection of rights…seeks a different balance between individual rights and collective interests. This balance is also at play in the operation of rights that are intended to recognize minority communities and enhance their vitality" (ibid). Here it is worth noting that Justice McLachlin either ignored or was unaware of Isaiah Berlin's argument that amelioration of any form of misery arising from natural or social causes cannot be brought about by a diminution or sacrifice of individual freedom. This is the logical fallacy of those, including judges in a liberal democracy such as Canada, who view the good secured by measures taken to advance equality in society outweighs, if need be, any sacrifice imposed on individual freedom. The reasoning is flawed since "a sacrifice is not an increase in what is being sacrificed, namely freedom, however great the moral need or the compensation for it. Everything is what it is: *liberty* is *liberty*, not *equality* or *fairness* or *justice* or *culture*, or human *happiness* or a quiet *conscience*" (Berlin: 125; italics added).

V.

It might be said freedom of speech is the "mother of all freedoms" and in its absence or limitation all other freedoms are wanting. The struggle in establishing freedom of speech as the foundation upon which eventually liberal democracy was constructed goes back several centuries. The English poet John Milton's *Areopagitica* prepared in 1644 is one of the most impassioned arguments made against censorship of books, and it has come to be read as among the most influential defences of freedom of speech.

In Milton's time formal censorship became a regular institution, the practice begun in the fifteenth century as the art of printing multiplied swiftly the publication of books. As books became widely available, religious and political authorities became fearful of ideas available to people for questioning them. Rulers backed by ecclesiastical authority, in Catholic realms that of the Church-led Inquisition, sought to contain the spread of "wrongful" ideas through books by licensing printing presses. This was the age of Reformation and Counter-Reformation, of the struggle to emancipate the Christian religion from the shackles of unreason and reconcile revelation with new discoveries made by men of science, and in this struggle the right to free speech was considered a key weapon. In *Areopagitica* Milton unleashed the full force of his reasoning for unlicensed printing so that ideas free of censorship might contend openly and assist in the reform of the Christian faith and church. He wrote:

If every action which is good, or evill in man at ripe years, were to be under pittance and prescription and compulsion, what were vertue but a name, what praise could be then due to well-doing, what grammercy to be sober, just, or continent? Many there be that complain of divin Providence for suffering *Adam* to transgresse. Foolish tongues! When God gave him reason, he gave him freedom to choose, for reason is but choosing; he had bin else a meer artificiall *Adam*, such an *Adam* as he is in the motions. We our selves esteem not of that obedience or love or gift, which is of force: God therefore left him free, set before him a provoking object, ever almost in his eyes; herein consisted his merit, herein the right of his reward, the praise of his abstinence (1898: 25).

Milton travelled in Europe, and met with Galileo "grown old, a prisner to the Inquisition, for thinking in Astronomy otherwise then the Franciscan and Dominican licencers thought" (ibid: 35). He declaimed, "Give me the liberty to know, to utter, and to argue freely according to conscience, above all liberties" (ibid: 50). And Milton offered what has come to be known as the "winds of doctrine" defence against censorship believing that truth can prevail despite any assistance of the censors. He wrote:

And though all the windes of doctrin were let loose to play upon the earth, so Truth be in the field, we do injuriously by licencing and prohibiting to misdoubt her strength. Let her and Falsehood grapple; who ever knew Truth put to the wors in a free and open encounter? ...For who knows not that Truth is strong next to the Almighty? She needs no policies, no stratagems, nor licencings to make her victorious; those are the shifts and the defences that error uses against her power (ibid: 51-52).

Milton's appeal for freedom of speech was connected to his theology based on the conviction that each individual was bound by his own conscience in worshipping God as he saw fit. It was an appeal that resonated with the English philosopher John Locke, Milton's younger contemporary. Locke published in 1689 *Letter on Toleration* while living in exile in Holland as the conflict between Catholics and Protestants deepened, and the Catholic monarch of France, Louis XIV, sought to crush the Protestant Huguenot Church in his realm and beyond. Locke's *Letter* followed later by his *Essay on Toleration* were pleas addressed to a sovereign responsible for maintaining civil order, and where he advanced the notion that the duty of subjects to obey passively should not be confused with their right to hold religious beliefs at variance with that of the ruler. In discussing Locke a contemporary thinker writes, "Human belief cannot submit to the claims of authority; and it cannot be true for any human being that he has good reason to abandon his own beliefs about what God requires of him at the command of another human being" (Dunn 2003: 33). The right of free speech — derived from the argument that man's belief in and relationship with God cannot be dictated by any authority — and tolerance for dissenting opinions to end religious conflicts were not utilitarian in origin. But the eventual success of Reformation established the principle of free speech as the central pillar of liberalism and liberal democracy.

Two centuries after Milton free speech found its most able advocate and defender in John Stuart Mill with the publication in 1859 of *On Liberty*. In her introductory essay to the Penguin edition of Mill's celebrated work, Gertrude Himmelfarb noted there were prominent thinkers, predecessors and contemporaries of Mill, who had written on the subject. There were, she wrote, "Adam Smith, the Founding Fathers, Paine and Godwin, Emerson and Thoreau, Proudhon and Stirner. Each celebrated liberty in one fashion or another, to one degree or another. But it remained for Mill to convert the idea of liberty into a philosophically respectable doctrine, to put it in its most comprehensive, extensive, and systematic form, the form in which it is generally known and accepted today" (1974: 9).

The making of the new world politically speaking took a huge leap forward with the American and French revolutions in the second half of the eighteenth century. Governments to be legitimate henceforth needed to be representative, democratically elected and limited. The idea of democracy spread, and what was once, for a very long time, held in suspicion (or worse, derided), became respectable. One Canadian political philosopher observed,

Democracy used to be a bad word. Everybody who was anybody knew that democracy, in its original sense of rule by the people or government in accordance with the will of the bulk of the people, would be a bad thing — fatal to individual freedom and to all the graces of civilized living. That was the position taken by pretty nearly all men of intelligence from the earliest historical times down to about a hundred years ago. Then within fifty years, democracy became a good thing (Macpherson: 1).

In Britain the Great Reform Act of 1832 initiated steps for reforming parliament by extending the franchise to newer groups of people in newly emerging factory towns. There were demands for dealing with rotten boroughs, for ending corrupt practices in electing members to the parliament, and for the House of Commons to become more democratically representative of the people.   But there was an undeniable dark side to democratic rule that appeared ominous to one of its first and most insightful chroniclers. In his classic work *Democracy in America* Tocqueville analyzed democracy's inherent tendency towards the "tyranny of the majority." In volume one, part two, of *Democracy* Tocqueville warned how the nature of majoritarian democratic rule based on popular opinion might threaten, impoverish and ostracize minorities and minority opinion.

    Though Alexis de Tocqueville (1805-59) was aristocratic by birth, philosophically he was a liberal and prized the right of an individual to live and think independently without coercion. He saw democracy as an irresistible force and he believed, as Raymond Aron commented on his work, democracy was "justified by the fact that it strove for the well-being of the greatest number; but this well-being would be without brilliance or grandeur, and it would always be attended by risks" (1968: 259). Tocqueville feared the "omnipotence of the majority" — a majority that "lives in perpetual adoration of itself" (2000: 245) — and is susceptible to demagogy. He wrote:

When a man or a party suffers from an injustice in the United States, whom do you want him to address? Public opinion? that is what forms the majority; the legislative body? it represents the majority and obeys it blindly; the executive power? it is named by the majority and serves as its passive instrument; the public forces? the public forces are nothing other than the majority in arms; the jury? the jury is the majority vested with the right to pronounce decrees: in certain states, the judges themselves are elected by the majority. Therefore, however iniquitous or unreasonable is the measure that strikes you, you must submit to it (ibid: 241).

Under such circumstances freedom of thought, in Tocqueville's view, was greatly inhibited by the majority popular opinion. "In America," he observed, "the majority draws a formidable circle around thought. Inside those limits, the writer is free; but unhappiness awaits him if he dares to leave them. It is not that he has to fear an auto-da-fé, but he is the butt of mortifications of all kinds and of persecutions every day" (ibid: 244). Tocqueville's study of democracy in America led him to make the prediction:

If ever freedom is lost in America, one will have to blame the omnipotence of the majority that will have brought minorities to despair and have forced them to make an appeal to material force. One will then see anarchy, but it will have come as a consequence of despotism (ibid: 249).

John Stuart Mill (1806-73) was Tocqueville's contemporary and his friend. Mill wrote long reviews in praise of Tocqueville's work. But Mill did not share Tocqueville's pessimism about the inherent tendency in democracy that works towards the tyranny of the majority. Mill was more sanguine about the mechanics of representative government than his friend, more confident that the finer minds in society elected to office would hold the balance between majority opinion, or the will of the people, and what is for the good of the society in terms of freedom and democracy. This required that the society remain open to dissenting views and opinions as Mill insisted in *On Liberty*, and to embrace without qualification the idea of freedom as the foundation of good society. Yet Mill, despite his optimism about representative government, eventually acknowledged the validity of Tocqueville's fear and came to view the tyranny of the majority as being located in the broadest sense within society itself. The struggle for liberty, therefore, was an unending opposition to society's tendency to set itself as the judge of rights and wrongs over individuals. According to Mill:

Like other tyrannies, the tyranny of the majority was at first, and is still vulgarly, held in dread, chiefly as operating through the acts of the public authorities. But reflecting persons perceived that when society is *itself the tyrant* — society collectively over the separate individuals who compose it — its means of tyrannizing are not restricted to the acts which it may do by the hands of its political functionaries. Society can and does execute its own mandates; and if it issues wrong mandates instead of right, or any mandates at all in things with which it ought not to meddle, it practises a *social tyranny* more formidable than many kinds of political oppression, since, though not usually upheld by such extreme penalties, it leaves fewer means of escape, penetrating much more deeply into the details of life, and enslaving the soul itself. Protection, therefore, against the tyranny of the magistrate is not enough; there needs protection also against the tyranny of the prevailing opinion and feeling, against the tendency of society to impose, by other means than civil penalties, its own ideas and practices as rules of conduct on those who dissent from them; to fetter the development and, if possible, prevent the formation of any individuality not in harmony with its ways, and compel all characters to fashion themselves upon the model of its own. *There is a limit to the legitimate interference of collective opinion with individual independence; and to find that limit, and maintain it against encroachment, is as indispensable to a good condition of human affairs as protection against political despotism* (1974: 63; italics added).

The one antidote to tyranny upon which rests all subsequent measures to protect and secure freedom that Mill came to emphasize, as Milton had done, was defending "Liberty of thought, from which it is impossible to separate the cognate liberty of speaking and of writing" (ibid: 74). But whereas Milton's appeal against censorship was grounded on his theology, Mill renewed Milton's "winds of doctrine" defence in support of freedom of speech on the basis of the utilitarian principle that what is good cannot be advanced through any form of censorship in society for certainty of any opinion might only be arrived at through subjecting it to the most rigorous test. In words that might not be improved upon, Mill wrote:

Strange it is that men should admit the validity of the arguments for free discussion, but object to their being 'pushed to an extreme', not seeing that unless the reasons are good for an extreme case, they are not good for any case. Strange that they should imagine that they are not assuming infallibility when they acknowledge that there should be free discussion on all subjects which can possibly be *doubtful*, but think that some particular principle or doctrine should be forbidden to be questioned because it is so *certain*, that is, because *they are certain* that it is certain. To call any proposition certain, while there is anyone who would deny its certainty if permitted, but who is not permitted, is to assume that we ourselves, and those who agree with us, are the judges of certainty, and judges without hearing the other side (ibid: 81; italics given).

Only and only when freedom of speech or "liberty of action" of an individual in society causes harm to another then, Mill conceded, is it warranted to limit freedom. The "only purpose for which power can be rightfully exercised over any member of a civilized community, against his will," he stated categorically, "is to prevent harm to others" (ibid: 68). And, moreover, he indicated implicitly and simply that respect for freedom of speech must be the criterion by which a community is considered civilized.

In defending the principle of freedom of speech Mill set forth his own *credo* and, by extension, he also set forth the ideal of a liberal society. Mill was an individualist and, as Gertrude Himmelfarb noted, "a laissez-fairist, and while he admitted exceptions to that doctrine (most notably to provide for compulsory education and to prohibit the marriage of those without the means of supporting a family) he admitted them as exceptions rather than the rule" (1974: 48). Interestingly *On Liberty* was published in the middle years of the nineteenth century when, according to the historian A.J.P. Taylor, England came closest to realizing the ideals of free-market economy and individual liberty with the minimum interference of the state or its power in display over the lives of the English people. In the years since then — 2009 marked the one hundred and fiftieth anniversary of *On Liberty*'s publication — the power of the states, fuelled by advances in science and technology, has increased substantially and demonstrably in controlling societies and limiting freedom of individuals.

VI.

The history of the last century could be read as one in which there was an unremitting squeeze on the limits of individual freedom around the world. In accepting the notion that *equality* mattered more than *liberty* liberals gave ground to forces in society at best suspicious of, if not hostile to, the notion of freedom. If there was any one society where individual freedom and freedom of speech remained somewhat protected in a century of revolutions, wars, genocides and glorification of totalitarian rule it was and remains the United States of America. The American exceptionalism is a tribute to the founding fathers of the republic and the constitution they provided for it. The first 10 Amendments to the constitution adopted in December 1791, and known as the "Bill of Rights", placed limits on the reach of governments to protect unalienable individual rights. The most famous amendment, the First Amendment, contains fourteen precious words stating "Congress shall make no law...abridging the freedom of speech, or of the press."

There is generally a gap between what is intended and what gets done, and politics in America has not been much different in this respect than that to be found elsewhere. Though the First Amendment protected free speech, what was meant by free speech was at first limited. Anthony Lewis's remarkable little book on the "biography" of the First Amendment — *Freedom for the Thought That We Hate* — traces how the idea and principle of freedom of speech evolved from the thinking of the founding fathers to the decisions of the Supreme Court justices over nearly two centuries. According to one scholar of the American constitution, while the judges are responsible for protecting the Bill of Rights their understanding by necessity has reflected the prevalent opinion of the society, and it is against such opinions that incrementally they have pressed forward to broaden and advance the meaning of the First Amendment right. He writes:

In the Supreme Court's early decisions there was little effort to spell out a "philosophy" of free speech. At the beginning of the twentieth century the Court had a fairly limited idea of what was protected by the rights of free speech, free press, and assembly and did not fully accept the ideas of John Stuart Mill. Over time, however, the Court's concept of what these rights encompassed expanded. Decade after decade the Court changed its mind, and what was not worthy of protection under the First Amendment a few years before was suddenly found to be covered by the amendment (McWhirter: 5).

Yet even with the First Amendment it is understood freedom of speech is· not absolute in the United States. The government, or the executive branch, has to convince the Supreme Court justices why any limitation it wants meets the requirement of "clear and present danger" in averting revolution and violence. It was Justice Oliver Wendell Holmes who famously used those words — "clear and present danger" — in writing for a unanimous Supreme Court decision in the case *Schenck v. United States* (1919). Holmes wrote:

We admit that in many places and in ordinary times the defendants in saying all that was said in the circular would have been within their constitutional rights. But the character of every act depends upon the circumstances in which it is done...The most stringent protection of free speech would not protect a man falsely shouting fire in a theatre and causing a panic...The question in every case is whether the words used are used in such circumstances and are of such a nature as to create a clear and present danger that they will bring about the substantive evils that Congress has a right to prevent. It is a question of proximity and degree.

Since these words were written, the bar of what might constitute "clear and present danger" has been greatly raised by the Court, just as the requirement to show how imminent is the "proximity and degree" of potential violence that would require limiting free speech.

It remains to be seen, however, to what extent freedom of speech will remain protected in the post-9/11 world in the United States given the pressures of multiculturalism and political correctness across the West to censor speech that offends minorities. The "Rushdie affair" followed by the Danish cartoon controversy have shown that in America, despite the First Amendment, there is mounting pressure from those in society who have invested in multiculturalism and, consequently, seek to control, censor, or criminalize free speech that might be considered or construed to be racist, inflammatory or incitement to violence in keeping with the requirements of the doctrine of multiculturalism.

In a world where terrorism has become a political instrument of transnational organizations such as al Qaeda, or of states such as the Islamic Republic of Iran, or of political parties such as the Hizbullah in Lebanon, violence and the threat of violence is ever-present and increasingly an aspect of global politics. In these circumstances freedom of speech is paradoxically under an insidious threat that comes from self-censorship. The refusal of the mainstream media in America to publish the Danish cartoons is an example of this threat, and government cannot force the free press to publish what it fears publishing. The fear of causing offense to Muslims, or to any other minority group, has had a chilling effect on free discourse of ideas and opinions, and especially when it comes to discussions relating to Islam. When the Yale University Press insisted that Jytte Klausen's book, *The Cartoons That Shook the World*, would only be published without any of the Danish cartoons in question or any other depictions of Muhammad for fear of igniting some new violent response of Muslims, self-censorship by a premier university press endangered freedom of speech no less than if the government had muzzled the press without any credible basis of a "clear and present danger." The Yale University Press example was soon after repeated when the Metropolitan Museum of Art in New York quietly removed images of Muhammad from its Islamic art collection and let it be known it would not display them when exhibits from Muslim lands open for public viewing in 2011.[19]

Self-censorship, or pre-emptive censorship in a free society, is clearly an act of handing victory to those who do not believe in individual freedom, and freedom of speech in particular; and conceding the argument for shrinking the realm of freedom in favour of those who argue, as multiculturalists do, that tolerance in a world of diversity requires free speech is limited so as not to cause offense to others. It is obvious the effect of such an argument does nothing to advance freedom in closed or illiberal societies, while it diminishes freedom in a free society without any compensating positive social effect for anyone including minority groups. The irony with multiculturalism is that the demand for limiting free speech made on behalf of protecting minorities inverts Tocqueville's insight into the "tyranny of the majority" by subjecting the majority to the "tyranny of minority groups" exercised through the levers of a liberal democratic state.

The First Amendment remains a check on the "tyranny of minority groups" in the United States. The American Supreme Court

---

[19] I. Vincent, "'Jihad' jitters at Met: Mohammed art gone," *New York Post*, January 10, 2010.

has demonstrated that the principal of free speech is much too valuable to be punished by criminal law even when such speech is bigoted or motivated by hatred based on race, religion, or sex and made during the commission of a crime. In other words the penalty for a crime committed cannot be increased by adding to it punishment for what the defendant might have said that was "hateful" (McWhirter: 53). In this respect American exceptionalism is at odds with European democracies where "hate" speech is a criminal offense as it is in Canada.

The European view about the necessity for prosecuting "hate" speech might be explained by its history. The experiences with the rise of fascism and the barbarity of the Nazis, world wars and the Holocaust which might have been prevented if Hitler's words in *Mein Kampf* had been taken seriously and checked in time, have shaped the European view that free speech must be limited when it is indisputable that free speech causes offense to minority groups. Hence, denial of the Holocaust is a criminal offense and the case against David Irving, an English historian of notoriety imprisoned in Austria during 2006-07 on charges of Holocaust-denial for speeches made in that country, is instructive. The Italian-born journalist and writer, Oriana Fallaci, was awaiting trial for charges alleging her writings on Islam had offended Muslims when she died in 2006 in New York. And, similarly, the trial of Geert Wilders was on the charges against him for making allegedly hateful comments in the Netherlands about Islam that offended Muslims.

It is this European view about limiting free speech on the grounds of hate crime, contrary to the American view, that lends itself to giving credibility to the efforts of the Organization of the Islamic Conference at the United Nations in moving a non-binding General Assembly Resolution 62/154 of 18 December 2007 for "combating defamation of religions". Article 11 of this resolution *"Urges* States to take action to prohibit the advocacy of national, racial or religious hatred that constitutes incitement to discrimination, hostility or violence," and such prohibition then, if the resolution is adopted, would become a step in the direction to criminalize any discussion of religions, particularly Islam, that practitioners of those religions view as an insult to their beliefs. In the guise of preventing "negative stereotyping of religions" (article 2), the OIC effort is directed to limiting free speech and subjecting rights and freedoms mentioned in the UN Charter to the principles of the Islamic *shari'ah*. Once again, this effort of the OIC at the UN illustrates the argument that limiting free speech will unlikely have any positive effect within closed or illiberal societies — and just about every member of the OIC is illiberal and more or less a closed society — by improving the situation of religious minorities, while it would diminish freedom in liberal democracies where tolerance of others, especially minorities, is a civic virtue and a constitutional guarantee.

The squeeze on freedom of speech has not relaxed in the early years of the twenty-first century, while the doctrine of multiculturalism has provided a new layer of argument for limiting free speech. But to the extent that free speech is the key building block of liberal democracy there cannot be a chipping away at it without weakening the entire structure resting on it. Any curtailment of free speech is also an undermining of government legitimacy in a liberal democracy. For freedom of speech, as Ronald Dworkin reminds us, "is not just a special and distinctive emblem of Western culture that might be generously abridged or qualified as a measure of respect for other cultures that reject it, the way a crescent or menorah might be added to a Christian religious display. Free speech is a *condition* of legitimate government. Laws and policies are not legitimate unless they have been adopted through a democratic process, and a process is not democratic if government has prevented anyone from expressing his convictions about what those laws and policies should be."[20] Any policy, therefore, to safeguard or expand multiculturalism by limiting free speech becomes an assault on democracy and a step backward for a liberal society.

---

[20] R. Dworkin, "The Right to Ridicule," *The New York Review of Books*, March 23, 2006 (italics added).

Chapter Six

THE AFTERMATH OF 9/11 TERROR

I believe that international terrorism is a modern form of warfare against liberal democracies. I believe that it is both wrong and foolhardy for any democratic state to consider international terrorism to be "someone else's" problem. Liberal democracies must acknowledge that international terrorism is a "collective problem."

— Senator Henry "Scoop" Jackson (1912-83)

The striking feature that stands out about the well co-coordinated terrorist attacks on New York and Washington on September 11, 2001 is how unprepared and surprised the United States was by what occurred that late summer morning. Despite the immense amount of investment over the years in developing intelligence capabilities to forestall a surprise attack on the United States as the one that marked the "day of infamy," December 7, 1941, when the Japanese imperial navy struck at Pearl Harbor, nineteen young Arab and Muslim men belonging to al Qaeda succeeded in eluding capture to destroy the twin towers of New York's World Trade Center, damage one wing of the Pentagon in Washington and kill more people, 2,823 on American soil in one day than had ever occured in the country's history.[21] The work in explaining and understanding September 11 continues, but we do have an overview of that day's history and what brought it about in the "Final Report of the National Commission on Terrorist Attacks Upon

---

[21] T. Templeton and T. Lumley, "9/11 in numbers," *Guardian*, August 18, 2002.

the United States" or *The 9/11Commission Report* of July 2004. In their preface to the Report released to the public, the co-chairs of the National Commission appointed by the Congress and the President, Thomas Kean and Lee Hamilton, wrote:

We learned that the institutions charged with protecting our borders, civil aviation, and national security did not understand how grave this threat could be, and did not adjust their policies, plans and practices to deter or defeat it. We learned of fault lines within our government — between foreign and domestic intelligence, and between and within agencies. We learned of the pervasive problems of managing and sharing information across a large and unwieldy government that had been built in a *different era* to confront *different dangers* (2004: xvi; italics added).

The grave threat the commissioners referred to was described as follows:

We learned about an enemy who is sophisticated, patient, disciplined, and lethal. The enemy rallies broad support in the Arab and Muslim world by demanding redress of political grievances, but its hostility towards us and our values is limitless. Its purpose is to rid the world of *religious and political pluralism, the plebiscite, and equal rights for women*. It makes no distinction between military and civilian targets. *Collateral damage* is not in its lexicon (ibid; italics given and added).

In thirteen chapters with notes, references and bibliography running over 550 pages, the *Report* provides for one of the most comprehensive analyses of al Qaeda as the terrorist network, its leading personalities including Osama Bin Ladin, the founder, and Khalid Sheikh Mohammed, the master-mind behind 9/11. It discusses radical Islam and the ideology behind *Islamist* terrorism that makes for the "catastrophic threat at this moment in history" and what needs to be done by the United States, its allies and others to deter and defeat this new enemy against world order (ibid: 362-63).

But the *Report* repeatedly makes a distinction between Islam, the world religion, and Islamist terrorism; between the followers of Islam, the global Muslim community, and the militant activists as well as the core supporters-sympathizers of al Qaeda. The *Report* states:

Islam is not the enemy. It is not synonymous with terror. Nor does Islam teach terror. America and its friends oppose a perversion of Islam, not the great world faith itself. Lives guided by religious faith, including literal beliefs in holy scriptures, are common to every religion, and represent no threat to us (ibid: 363).

These words addressed the geopolitical reality of world politics in which the global presence of Islam and the Muslim community loom ever larger. The 2009 Pew Research Center's study on world Muslim population indicates that there are 1.57 billion Muslims "representing 23% of an estimated 2009 world population of 6.8 billion" (2009a). From a policy perspective, as the Report was primarily concerned with, it was essential that a critical distinction be made and kept between Islam and Islamist terrorism. To keep this distinction front and center was vital so that there might not be any public confusion resulting from the "war on terror" President George W. Bush launched soon after 9/11 against al Qaeda and the Taliban regime in Afghanistan and regime change in Baghdad, that the United States was not at war against Islam and Muslims.

The effort to keep in perspective the distinction between Islam and Islamist terrorism in public discussions became the hallmark of the U.S. government and its agencies, the corporate media and the academia, and the same has been the effort by most Western governments and societies. But this effort comes at a price. The likelihood of any analysis that showed Islam, the faith, was not *historically-speaking* at a distance from organized violence and terror, and that the war within Islam going back to its earliest years in Medina soon after Muhammad, the prophet, passed away in 632, has provided the template for Islamist terrorism of al Qaeda variety in recent years, were at best to be shunned. The reasoning behind such a view is driven by the strategic interests of the West given the geopolitical reality of Islam and Muslims. All the terrorist-hijackers on 9/11 were Arabs, most were of Saudi Arabian and Yemeni origin, and this was representative of the larger demography of Islamist-terrorists that showed the overwhelming number of activists comes from Saudi Arabia, followed by Yemen, together making up ninety percent of Al Qaeda fighters, while the balance, ten percent, originate in the rest of the Muslim world (National Commission: 232). Saudi Arabia as the largest oil-producer with the largest proven oil-reserve in the world has been the closest ally of Britain, and then the United States, from its founding years in the early 1920s. The bitterest adversary of the United States and the West in the Muslim world is the Islamic Republic of Iran on the Persian Gulf. But Iranians were not involved in the events of 9/11 and, because of the Sunni-Shi'ite split within the Muslim world, Islamist activists of al Qaeda look upon Iranian Shi'ites as a sectarian enemy. Sunni Islamist terrorism is primarily a phenomenon of Arab Islam fuelled by Arab petrodollars. But the United States and other Western democracies owing to the demands of oil politics bent backwards to distinguish between Islam and Islamist terrorism. This was done to save the West's relationship with the Arab Middle East, and give diplomatic cover to Saudi Arabia, or the House of Saud, following the attacks on the heartland of America and those committed on European soil, in Madrid and London soon after 9/11.

The terrorist attacks of 9/11 and after did not ignite any overt hostility in the United States, or broadly speaking in the West, against Muslims. A rolling survey between 2002 and 2009 by the Pew Research Center found that Americans with higher levels of knowledge or familiarity with Islam and Muslims tended less to link violence with religion (2009b). A majority of Americans, including all branches of the government, refused to view Islam and Muslims through the lens of Islamist terror. In the larger perspective of comparative history six decades after Pearl Harbor when most Americans turned to view Japanese-Americans as enemy-suspect and the government rounded them up for detention, the response following 9/11 in respect to Islam and Muslims in America illustrated the immense changes that had occurred in society. America had become multiethnic, and multiculturalism had taken hold of the country where its "white" or European racial profile of the population is in historic decline from a high of 87 percent in 1970 down to 66 percent in 2008.[22] The probable long term effect of such demographic change and multiculturalism, according to one analyst, for America's domestic and foreign policy is predictable. McConnell writes:

American foreign policy will necessarily become less ambitious, more a product of horse-trading between ethnic groups. Messianism, in either its

---

[22] S. McConnell, "Not So Huddled Masses: Multiculturalism and Foreign Policy," *World Affairs,* Spring 2009, available online (www.worldaffairsjournal.org).

Protestant or neoconservative variants, will be part of America's past, not its future. Americans will not conceive of themselves as orchestrators of a benevolent global hegemony, or as agents of an indispensable nation. Schlesinger, for one, exaggerated the extent of the fall when he averred that a foreign policy based on "careful balancing of ethnic constituencies" was suitable only for secondary powers, like the late Austrian-Hungarian empire. But he exaggerated only slightly (ibid).

In Europe, and in Canada, the effect of multiculturalism in domestic and foreign policy became more deeply entrenched than in America during the same period, and the majority population remains more accommodating of Islam and Muslims as part of their multiethnic population as it is of other non-European cultures and faith traditions. Consequently, there is great reluctance in the mainstream of European and North American societies to explore any possible connection between Islam and Islamist violence.

II.

Once the initial horror over the events of 9/11 faded, and the Bush administration launched its "war on terror" the expected debate over how to explain terrorist violence got launched across the West. The critics of the United States' foreign policy, predominantly belonging to the liberal-left of the intellectual class, were quick to establish the argument that terrorism whether emanating from the Middle East or elsewhere was the organized response of the poor and the oppressed people to injustices real or perceived in large parts of the developing world. This explained terrorism on the basis of "root cause" analysis. The proponents of the "root cause" argument mounted a campaign that was a reminder of those who readily "blame America first" irrespective of what is at issue.

The "root cause" explanation of 9/11 shifts responsibility from the Islamist terrorists to the socioeconomics of capitalist-imperialism; it points to the consequences of the wars of plunder and conquest launched by the West against indigenous populations in both the New and the Old World, and which continue to the benefit of the United States as the most powerful imperialist or hegemonic power in world history. This is the Noam Chomsky "school" of political thinking with a global following of "radical" or "revolutionary" intellectuals and activists. The attraction of "Chomsky-ism" is the readily packaged reductive formula Chomsky provides in explaining contemporary world history as one unending assault by the powerfully organized military-industrial centre of world capitalism — represented by the United States in modern times — against those people and cultures resistant to the hegemony of this centre. Chomsky's 1993 book, *Year 501: The Conquest Continues*, was published to coincide with the 500th anniversary of Christopher Columbus's voyage of 1492, and it is an example of his writing that has made him hugely popular among the Third World experts, liberal-left intellectuals, supporters of multiculturalism, and Islamists and their friends. Edward Said added his voice as a high profile Arab (Palestinian)-American public intellectual to the Chomsky "school" of blaming the United States for conditions that make for political despair resulting in terrorism. Said, as quoted by Rashid Khalidi, wrote:

We are in for many more years of turmoil and misery in the Middle East, where one of the main problems is, to put it as plainly as possible, American power. What America refuses to see clearly, it can hardly hope to remedy (2004: 152).

The list of writers, activists, journalists, academics and politicians who have written on or spoken about 9/11 in terms set by Chomsky and Said is long. Among Canadians Linda McQuaig, journalist and author, is representative of those insistent on "root cause" explanation. Following the terrorist bombings in London in July 2005, Linda McQuaig wrote "terrorism is actually a response to military interventions perpetrated by western governments."[23] In terms of multiculturalism, the "root cause" explanation stands in the way of those asking hard and critical questions of a religion and culture from whose midst Islamist terrorists emerged.

---

[23] L. McQuaig, "Terror Attacks Are Response to Military Actions," *Toronto Star*, July 31, 2005.

III.

Islamist terrorism and the ideology that promotes it, Islamism or radical Islam, is not an alien off-shoot within Islamic or Muslim history. It is instead a mutation of a violent strain of Muslim religious-thought and practice that might be traced back to the earliest years of Islam, and which was in part responsible for deepening inter-tribal and sectarian violence soon after the demise of Muhammad in 632 (Mansur: 1-9). The basis of radical Islam is in the binary thinking of its proponents, that the world is divided into two warring halves of those who accept the fundamentals of Islam and act upon them to establish society accordingly, and those who reject Islam. In recent years such thinking resurfaced in political movements within the Muslim world opposing the modern secular world and its values, and seeking a return to the form of rulership closely associated with Muhammad and his closest companions established in the first decades of seventh century Arabia.

For Islamists, or jihad-ists — (from the Arabic word *jihad* meaning effort or struggle, including the use of violence as "means" to achieve religiously defined "ends") — there is no separation of religion and politics; instead religion is politics and national identity and the purpose of their struggle is to reconstruct the ideal of Islamic rule in the here and now. Muslim faith in its bare essentials is affirmation of the Oneness of God and of Muhammad as the Messenger bearing the final revelation that is contained in the Qur'an. The ideal system of authority, Muslims believe, was given its basic form by the Prophet of Islam in the city of Medina where he lived during the final decade of his life; it was inherited by his companions described as the *al-khilafat ar-rasul allah* (the Successor of the Prophet) and known in history as the Caliphate, and where the rule of law or *shari'ah* is based on the Qur'an and *hadith*, the traditions of the Prophet. Muslims very early in the history of Islam came to disagree over the practical method and the nature of legitimate authority in working this ideal system, and on how to construct it, protect it, and spread it in a world in which they insisted religion and politics were inseparable. The tradition-bound pre-modern world of Islam eventually was surpassed by Europe from the sixteenth century onwards. In the centuries since then the world of Islam was affected by the social revolutions and political upheavals in Europe, by the rise and spread of European colonialism and imperialism, and by the ideas and inventions that gave birth to the modern world.

The world of Islam is not monolithic, and the responses of Muslims to developments around them have been varied over time and circumstances from seeking reconciliation with the imperatives of the modern world in terms of science and democracy, to resisting and rejecting the modern world as alien and hostile to Islam. It is within this context of modern history that Islamism was elaborated during the last century by its founders — Hasan al-Banna (1906-49) and Sayyid Qutb (1903-66) from Egypt, and Sayyid Abul A'la Mawdudi (1903-79) from Pakistan — as a modern ideological response to the political and social challenges faced by Muslims. These Islamist thinkers revived the strain of thought within Islam that prioritized jihad conceived as the Islamic version of "just war" to establish and maintain the rule of *shari'ah* in history after the age of Salaf (the first three generation of earliest Muslims who were companions of the Prophet or most proximate to him in time) ended. The Muslim thinker credited most for putting together the fundamentals of jihadist thinking is Ibn Taymiyya from the thirteenth century. According to Mary Habeck, author of *Knowing the Enemy: Jihadist Ideology and the War on Terror*, "The modern Islamists and jihadists alike assert that they draw their primary inspiration from Ibn Taymiyya, a widely respected interpreter of the Qur'an and sunna (prophetic tradition)." Habeck explains:

It was Ibn Taymiyya who persuasively argued that Islam requires state power, the foundational principle for all Islamists. Living at a time when shamanist Mongols had conquered the core of the Islamic world, he issued religious rulings which decreed that Muslims could not live in a nation ruled by infidels. A more complicated situation was presented by Mongol rulers who claimed to be Muslims and yet continued to use their native system of laws — the *yasa* — to make judgments. Ibn Taymiyya asserted that these rulers were acting immorally and contrary to the Qur'anic text, which said that Muslims were only truly the "best community" when they "enjoined the good and forbade the evil." This injunction he took to mean that Muslims had to follow and implement all the commandments, both positive and negative, laid down by God and explained by Muhammad (and as interpreted by legal experts); not the least of them could be ignored or disobeyed. Ibn Taymiyya argued that since the Mongol rulers failed to carry out the entire shari`a of God and even pretended that their own system of law was superior in certain regards, they were not fulfilling this key requirement. Such rulers were clearly infidels and not Muslims at all, and as unbelievers had to be fought and killed (2006: 19-20).

In the eighteenth century Muhammad bin Abd al-Wahhab, a native of Nejd in the eastern portion of the Arabian peninsula, revived the teachings of Ibn Taymiyya and preached opposition to the Ottoman rulers with their capital in Istanbul (ancient Constantinople) deemed corrupt. Abd al-Wahhab made alliance with a local tribal leader, Muhammad bin Sa`ud, and pushed his rigidly puritanical movement — it is also viewed by many as a quasi-reformist movement — against tribes in the interior of the Arabian peninsula that refused to acknowledge him as a religious leader. In the late nineteenth and early twentieth century the Wahhabi-Saudi alliance was revived by Abd al-Aziz ibn Sa`ud, a descendant of Muhammad bin Sa`ud. Ibn Sa`ud (as he would be known) went on to establish the Kingdom of Saudi Arabia with Wahhabism as its official doctrine after World War I with the support of Britain (Algar, 2002; Schwartz, 2002).

The modern founders of Islamism — Banna, Qutb, Mawdudi — influenced by the currents of fascist and totalitarian ideologies of their time in the rise of Nazi Germany and Communist Russia updated the teachings of Ibn Taymiyya and Abd al-Wahhab in launching revivalist movements for the establishment of *shari'ah*-based states. Their writings were instrumental in gaining activists while consolidating the Islamist agenda of the Muslim Brotherhood in Egypt and the neighbouring Arab lands, and Jama'at al-Islami in Pakistan. They opposed modernizing rulers in the world of Islam, demanded the establishment of *shari'ah* legislation as the basis of religio-political order in Muslim majority countries following independence from European colonialism after World War II, denounced secular and liberal democracy in any form, and called for war in support of Palestine and the elimination of the Jewish state of Israel. The Shi'ite minority sect in Islam with a majority following within Iran developed religio-political thinking parallel to Islamism among the majority Sunni population of the Muslim world. In 1979 Ayatollah Khomeini, the exponent of the Shi'ite version of Islamism, emerged as the leader of the Islamic revolution in Iran to topple the Shah and replace the monarchical order with an Islamic Republic.

Through the Cold War years (1946-91) the Western powers led by the United States came to view Islamism, despite its counter-revolutionary revivalist ideology and virulent opposition to Israel, as an ally against international Communism. As petrodollars flowed into the coffers of Saudi Arabia the Wahhabi-influenced rulers of the Kingdom where the two holiest cities of Islam, Mecca and Medina, are located became the favourite Arab ally of Washington in the Middle East. When the former Soviet Union invaded and occupied Afghanistan in 1979, President Ronald Reagan and his administration seized the strategic opportunity to supply weaponry to Afghan *mujahideen* (freedom-fighters) with funds provided by Saudi Arabia and shipped through Pakistan. The covert Afghan war attracted Islamists from Arab-speaking countries, and once the Soviet Union withdrew in February 1989 Afghanistan rapidly descended into internal conflict among warlords until the Taliban, an Islamist movement logistically trained and supplied by the Pakistan's military intelligence, gained control in the mid-1990s (Rashid, 2001). Despite warning signs of troubles the West ignored Afghanistan once the war against the Soviet occupation ended. But Islamist fighters stayed behind, and sometime in 1996 Osama bin Laden with his band of followers moved into this conflict-ridden country from Sudan and set up there the headquarters for al Qaeda with support from the Taliban leader Mullah Umar.

From Afghanistan the activists of al Qaeda prepared and launched the terrorist strikes of 9/11 on New York and Washington, and infiltrated existing Muslim organizations around the world. Osama bin Laden succeeded in intensifying the jihad inside the world of Islam and made it go global (Ruthven, 2002). He tapped into the teachings of the modern founders of Islamism, drew upon the traditional language of Ibn Taymiyya, built upon the experience of the Afghan mujahideen, incorporated the grievances of the swollen population of the Muslim world against their corrupt rulers, denounced the presence of the United States in Saudi Arabia and its support for Israel in "occupying" Muslim Palestine and Jerusalem, and then declared war against what he labeled a "Judeo-Christian Crusader alliance" in control of Muslim lands and its resources. Any objective assessment of Osama bin Laden will take into account how he succeeded beyond the imagination of the modern founders of Islamism to precipitate a collision between the world of Islam and the West. He was militarily defeated, driven into the high mountains of the Hindu Kush and presumed most likely dead. But nearly a decade after the most ingenious and daring terrorist operation mounted by al Qaeda that destroyed the Twin Towers of the World Trade Center in New York City, Osama bin Laden was found by the U.S. intelligence. He was living, as it was revealed, for quite sometime in the northern military town of Abbottabad in Pakistan, and in a highly successful commando operation carried out by the U.S. Navy SEALS on May 1, 2011 Osama bin Laden was killed, his body flown to a U.S. aircraft carrier in the Arabian Sea and dumped overboard.[24] But it is unlikely, or too soon to be stated definitively, that the beast of Islamist terrorism Osama bin Laden unleashed against the West and its presence in Muslim lands, has been laid to rest as a result of his despatch.

IV.

Long before anyone in the West heard of Osama bin Laden, the ideas of the modern founders of Islamism found their way from the Middle East into Europe and North America. The post-1945 wave of immigration from the Old World to the New brought Muslims in increasing numbers, and with them came the culture and politics of the world of Islam. Multiculturalism provided Muslim immigrants — as it did to others from other non-European cultural backgrounds such as Sikhs from Punjab, Hindus from India and the Indian diaspora in the Caribbean and East Africa, Africans and Chinese — the comfort of not demanding assimilation into the majority white Caucasian society and encouragement to cultivate their own religious traditions. Mosques sprang up in just about every Western town and city where sufficient numbers of Muslim families settled, and mosque related institutions became the centre for social activities of Muslim immigrants. By the end of the last century the second and third generations of Muslim immigrants, either born in the West or having arrived at a very young age, became more visible and confident to engage in politics outside their communities, and to push for acceptance of their religiously

---

[24] P. Baker, H. Cooper and M. Mazzetti, "Bin Laden is Dead, Obama Says," *New York Times*, May 1, 2011.

defined political views as held by the majority of Muslims. The politics of the Middle East and South Asia got imported into Muslim communities in the West, and it was only a matter of time before major political parties began paying closer attention to the wishes of Muslim immigrants for electoral purposes.

The Islamist zealots are a minority within the world of Islam, but the politics of Islamism resonate widely among Muslims and it can be said that most of the Muslim majority countries accept in principle the fundamental Islamist demand of adopting *shari'ah* as the basis of legislation. This "unofficial" or tacit acceptance of the Islamist demand was illustrated at the Cairo conference in August 1990 of the Organization of Islamic Conference where member states issued the "Cairo Declaration on Human Rights in Islam." The Cairo Declaration spelled out the OIC view on human rights as a parallel and complementary "official" statement to stand alongside the 1948 UN Declaration of Human Rights. But for OIC members, hence the world of Islam, the Cairo Declaration — article 25 of the Declaration stated the "Islamic Shari'ah is the only source of reference for the explanation or clarification to any of the articles of this Declaration" — takes precedence. This meant Muslim immigrants in the West were under advice by their religious leaders that in situations of conflict between the principles enunciated in the UN Declaration of Human Rights and the Cairo Declaration they adhere to the latter; and from this it followed that Muslims engage politically to bring their host Western governments recognize *shari'ah* and make, allowance for them to live in accordance with its provisions. The push for *shari'ah* recognition in family law as part of the multicultural arrangement in the West has become one of the key objectives of immigrant Muslim activists, and as the Muslim immigrant population grows in numbers the mainstream political parties have also become increasingly receptive to the idea.

Similarly, Muslim immigrants began to push for changes in the foreign policy of Western governments to be more accommodating of Muslim views on the Arab-Israeli conflict, and Muslim support for Kashmiri Muslims in India. Here again the majority Muslim opinion has been greatly influenced by the Islamist perspective, and Muslims by a huge majority unquestioningly adopted the view that the establishment of Israel by partitioning "Arab land" (Palestine) was illegitimate. While the Arab-Israeli conflict intensified over time and the rights of the Palestinians to have a state of their own gained international recognition, Muslim immigrants became receptive to the bigoted and hateful language Islamists use in defaming Jewish religion and history. Muslim anti-Semitism was given the cover of religious teachings of Islam, and in meeting little official disapproval of the Western governments has grown more strident in public.

By the time 9/11 occurred Islamism was firmly established within Muslim communities in the West. This also meant that shady subversive cells of Islamists had spread, and the mainstream Muslim organizations either based in the mosques or outside were sufficiently penetrated by Islamists to lend support politically and financially to promoting Islamism. Money has flowed liberally from Saudi Arabia and other oil-producing Middle Eastern states, such as Libya and Iran, into the coffers of Muslim immigrant communities in the West and Muslim organizations in the poorer Muslim societies of Asia and Africa to propagate Islamist doctrine and Wahhabism. It is estimated that in the period 1970-2003 as much as US$70 billion was distributed by the Saudi Wahhabi establishment for Islamist missionary work, and a portion of this money was directed to Europe and North America to build mosques and mosque-related schools for spreading Wahhabism in the immigrant Muslim communities (Allen, 2006; Alexiev, 2003; Ehrenfeld, 2005). The public face of religion provided cover for Islamists to recruit and organize for jihad. In *Cold Terror: How Canada Nurtures and Exports Terrorism Around the World* — a pioneering study on the subject — Stewart Bell described the extent to which Canada was penetrated by terrorist organizations and how some of the major terrorist groups, such as Hizbollah (partisans of God) based in Lebanon, established their presence in the country. The Canadian situation is no longer an exception in the West; it is, instead, more or less representative of the West that has greatly changed over the previous half-century with the making of the welfare state and the politics of multiculturalism. Bell writes:

Canada is the land of opportunity for terrorist groups seeking money to finance their bloody campaigns. Jobs are plentiful; welfare is generous. It is easy enough to set up a charity dedicated to a worthy humanitarian cause and launder the money to terrorist causes (2005: 4).

The terrorist attacks on New York and Washington on 9/11 would not have been the first strike in America's heartland if Ahmed Ressam, the "millennium bomber" of Algerian origin headed for Los Angeles to bomb the city's main airport, was not apprehended when attempting to cross from Canada into the United States in December 1999. Ressam entered Canada illegally and when detained claimed refugee status as a victim of the brutal civil war raging in Algeria during the 1990s (ibid: 147-55).

Terrorist cells within immigrant communities in Canada, as Bell described, raised concern about the possibility of "home-grown" terrorism mounted by children of immigrants. This concern turned real when young Muslim men born in England carried out the suicide bombings of the London transport system on July 7, 2005. A year later in June 2006 members of the Canadian security and intelligence services (CSIS) arrested eighteen young men in the Toronto area on charges of planning terrorist strikes in the country. The context was similar in both London and Toronto. Young Muslim men came of age in a multicultural society where pride in one's immigrant culture laid the grounds for absorbing the extremist ideology of Islamists and drove some young males to engage in terrorism. Ed Husain, a former Islamist, has written about his experiences as a child of immigrant Muslims in England and, like the London suicide-bomber of July 2007, he grew up in a community exposed to the virulent language of fundamentalist Muslims and Islamist ideology. He later repented, turned his back on Islamism, and described in *The Islamist* what his experiences can teach the majority population in the West of the perils of homegrown terrorism. According to Ed Husain,

The events of 7/7 did not occur in a vacuum. The suicide bombers were not trained in isolation, away from Britain, in Afghanistan and Pakistan. Long before the overthrow of Saddam Hussein in Iraq, in Britain's Muslim communities the ideas of a global jihad...and preparation for the all-powerful Islamist state were, and still are, accepted as normal and legitimate... Siddique Khan, the lead 7/7 suicide bomber, spoke of 'my people' as those in Iraq. He declared that he was 'at war' with Britain, and in this war he was 'a soldier'. Khan did not see fellow Brits as human brothers and sisters. I too once expressed such sentiments. The 7/7 suicide bombers were symptomatic of a deeper problem: unbridled Islamist ideology gaining a stronger hold in Britain's Muslim communities (2007: 277-78).

Melanie Phillips, a London-based author and journalist, described in *Londonistan* the growth and spread of immigrant communities as separate enclaves across Britain where they make homes having minimum social contacts with the majority population. Her account of the rise and spread of Muslim extremism in Britain exposed the unforeseen effects of multiculturalism. She writes:

The culture of separate groups replaced the universal vision of humanity in which all individuals shared the same national project on equal terms. By making such a fetish of the promotion of minority cultures as proof of Britain's antiracist virtue, it encouraged British Muslims to start campaigning for public recognition of their religious agenda by the state. As the writer Kenan Malik observed, by the late 1980s the focus of antiracist protest in Bradford had shifted from political issues, such as policing and immigration, to religious and cultural issues: a demand for Muslim schools and for separate education for girls, a campaign for halal meat in school, and the confrontation over *The Satanic Verses*. As different groups began asserting their identities ever more fiercely, so the shift from the political to the cultural arena helped create a more tribal society (2006: 68-9).

Multiculturalism was promoted as a policy that would make for a tolerant, accommodating and peaceful society tending towards increased diversity as a result of open-door immigration policy. But tolerance of the intolerant, the accommodation of those who push extremism of one sort or another as the Islamists or the Khalistani Sikhs have done, under the cover of multiculturalism has amounted to the undermining of liberal democracy from the inside. This is the paradox of liberal democracy, its vulnerability resulting from its concerns to improve the conditions of living for its citizens and its commitment to remain true to its own principles of freedom and individual rights even as some might want to subvert them.

V.

Multiculturalism's foundational principle that all cultures are of equal merit and deserve equal respect can be tested on two counts. First, by examining how any culture protects the right of individual and respects, as John Stuart Mill phrased it, "the inward domain of consciousness, demanding liberty of conscience in the most comprehensive sense" (1974: 71). Secondly, what is the status of women in any given culture.

No modern thinker has written as clearly and forcefully on liberty and what it means in the most fundamental sense of freedom of conscience and freedom of speech as did Mill. Most subsequent writings on the subject are footnotes or parenthetical circumlocutions of those who did not abandon the quest of abridging the fundamental right of free speech even as they present themselves as defenders of freedom on the ground, however tenuous or ill-conceived, of protecting the rights of others. At any time a government, even if it represents completely the will and opinion of the entire people under its rule, chooses to control the opinion of an individual it would be doing wrong as Mill contended. This power to coerce was illegitimate in Mill's view, and in *On Liberty* he wrote:

The best government has no more title to it than the worst. It is as noxious, or more noxious, when exercised in accordance with public opinion than when in opposition to it. *If all mankind minus one were of one opinion, mankind would be no more justified in silencing that one person than he, if he had the power, would be justified in silencing mankind* (1974: 76; italics added).

This is the liberal ideal, and the ground that must not be conceded to any argument that suggests the world could be made a better place if the opinion of one man judged to be outrageous by his peers is silenced. This ideal sets apart the liberal society from all other types of society where non-liberal or illiberal ideas prevail and freedom is merely what those with power limit it to be.

The record of governments through history is the regular abuse of the liberal ideal of freedom of conscience, and even by those governments as in our time in the West that claim to be of liberal persuasion. Instead of securing the principle of free speech as non-negotiable, proponents of multiculturalism have pushed for legislative means to trim this fundamental right on the grounds that freedom of speech cannot be a license for "irresponsible" speech or speech that promotes hatred towards some identifiable group. In some liberal societies of Europe, such as Holland and Britain, and in Canada this legislative effort to abridge freedom of speech has resulted in human rights legislations and establishing human rights industries, such as the Canadian Human Rights Commission.

The irony of the above in terms of multicultural sensibility has been to reinforce illiberal tendencies in most non-European immigrant cultures with their emphasis on collective over individual rights. The fate of Socrates — the most remarkable of free thinkers ever to have lived and, as Mill described him, "the man who probably of all then born had deserved the best of mankind" was put to death by the Athenian state for his opinions — stands as a warning of what might happen when freedom of conscience is subject to a vote or denounced as blasphemy. The death sentence pronounced by Iran's Ayatollah Khomeini for Salman Rushdie for writing *The Satanic Verses* considered blasphemous was a reminder once again how coercive and bloody-minded is the politics of those who detest freedom, and the length to which they will go in silencing an individual with whom they do not agree. The "Rushdie affair" divided people in the West between those who maintained Rushdie's right to freely express himself regardless of how Muslims or anyone else felt offended by his writings, and those who insisted that freedom of speech is not absolute especially when it offends religious or cultural sensibility of a people (Ruthven, 1990). To recall Socrates's fate in the context of the "Rushdie affair" confirms, if such confirmation was ever needed yet again, why freedom of speech must remain inviolate and protected from demands for its curtailment because someone or some group find what is said or written offensive to their taste, or belief, or whatever it is they hold dear. But the defence of the liberal ideal of free speech requires the sort of commitment — courage to defend an individual against group thinking — that is often lacking among contemporary liberals, especially those who have embraced the politics of multiculturalism. The "Rushdie affair" was the precedent for the effort Islamists mounted in 2006 to punish Denmark as a violent global uproar was engineered in protest of the cartoons of Muhammad published by the Danish newspaper *Jyllands-Posten* (Mansur: chap. 7).

Whatever the religious dictate in Islam on matters of individual conscience — the Qur'an is categorical in stating that "there is no compulsion in religion" (2:256) — the history of Muslims shows there is no allowance made for individual opinion that runs counter to that of men in power. There was little tolerance for the dissident view in Islam as it historically evolved from its seventh century Arabian setting and, once the brief flirtation of those Muslims who pushed for independent thinking on rational grounds — the Mutazilites in the eighth and ninth century Baghdad — was officially prohibited by the rulers and religious scholars, Islamic culture discouraged any innovation in religious thought as heresy. Ayatollah Khomeini's death sentence for Rushdie reminded the majority of Muslims everywhere — most Muslims supported in principle the religious-based ruling of the Iranian leader — how conceding to the idea of individual rights and freedom of speech might disrupt and undermine the belief of Muslims in their sacred texts, the Qur'an and the *hadith* (the collected traditions of Muhammad).

The culture of Muslim immigrants grounded on their religious belief stands in opposition to liberal values, the foremost being the freedom of conscience and the freedom of speech. It makes a mockery of multicultural piety that all cultures are of equal merit. Indeed, Muslims individually or as members of organizations have readily taken recourse to federal and provincial human rights commissions in Canada to punish and silence anyone writing critically of Islam and Muslims as they did in bringing complaints against Ezra Levant for publishing the Danish cartoons in his magazine *Western Standard* and against *Maclean's* and writer Mark Steyn for publishing material considered anti-Islamic.

By the standards of the first test of how cultures respect individual rights and freedom of conscience, it is evident the culture imported by immigrant Muslims — and not only Muslims since group identity and group loyalty are the common features of non-liberal cultures — into the West cannot be viewed as equal to Western liberal culture. When the second test pertaining to the status of women in different cultures is considered, the result for multiculturalism is as damaging as the first test.

Islamic culture is not exceptional or unique in viewing female sex as subordinate to the male sex. But what makes the Islamic culture stand out is the insistence of traditional-minded Muslims, and Islamists, that the unequal status of men and women in Islam is based on its sacred texts, the Qur'an and the *hadith*. This subordinate status of women to men, therefore, is unalterable and fixed for all time. The struggle for gender equality in Islam is old, and at one time during the early decades of the last century gains made by women in acquiring education and professional qualifications appeared irreversible. The Islamist backlash, however, has pushed back the gains made by women, and Muslim majority countries in Asia and Africa generally suffer from acute gender disparities in terms of education, health care and income compared to other non-European societies and documented, for instance, by the UN backed Arab Human Development Report (UNDP, 2002; Mernissi: chapters 1-2; Ahmed, 1992; El Saadawi, 1980). Muslim immigrants on arriving in the West discover the unsettling reality that the distinguishing feature of the European and North American societies is gender equality and the freedom for women in society. The collision between the culture of Muslim immigrants and Western culture is indicative of the politically incorrect reality that there is no equality between cultures that treat women differently. It is the voices of Muslim women or women of Muslim origin — voices of women such as Fatima Mernissi, Nawal El Sadaawi, Shirin Ebadi, Leila Ahmed, Wafa Sultan, Nonie Darwish, Taslima Nasrin, Ayaan Hirsi Ali, Azar Nafisi, Necla Kelek, Benazir Bhutto, Asma Jahangir, Samia Labidi and countless others from within the Muslim culture — that are most committed to disclose the inequities of gender relations among Muslims and the extent of misogyny that permeates Muslim countries and Muslim immigrant communities in the West.

The insistence based on multicultural thinking on treating all cultures as equal and deserving of equal respect in practical terms means cultural relativism, where the modern liberal culture is made to appear as no different from a culture in which individual freedom is constrained or missing and gender inequality prevails. Multiculturalism under such circumstances is an assault on the liberal culture of the West that has evolved independently over several centuries since the values of the Enlightenment took hold of Europe from at least the eighteenth century. Until 9/11 the politics of multiculturalism could be sustained on the fiction that immigrants in the West were more or less open to adopting the cultural values of the majority population if given time and encouragement without any pressure for discarding what would be dysfunctional aspects of their own cultures in the West. But since 9/11 what is undeniable is the extent to which Muslim immigrants, or a vocal segment among them, are unwilling to accept the culture of their adopted countries even as they push for accommodation of their imported non-liberal or illiberal culture that stands starkly in opposition to the cultural norms in the West. It is as if the exception is proving the rule, that Islam in general and Islamism in particular with its influence within the growing Muslim immigrant communities have rendered the politics of multiculturalism — as Bruce Bawer has catalogued in *Surrender: Appeasing Islam, Sacrificing Freedom* — complicit in gradually weakening the West's resolve to steadfastly hold to the principle of individual freedom that distinguishes it from the East.

Chapter Seven

THE PARADOX OF MULTICULTURALISM

Between 1967 and 2001 the tempo and substance of social change in the West was deeper and more intensive than in any period of similar length during the previous century. The list is long. The cumulative effect of the civil rights movement, the feminist revolution and the gay rights movement, anti-Vietnam War protests, revolutions in transportation and communications, the global spread of the market economy, the making of the worldwide web, the tearing down of the Berlin Wall, the unification of Europe, and the collapse of Soviet communism made liberal democracies in the West more open, accommodating and responsive to public demands. But the change that grew upon the West in these years and held the potential to affect politics adversely was the nature of immigration from the Third World countries to Europe and North America. The West in general and Western Europe in particular, during this period "became a multiethnic society in a fit of absence of mind" (Caldwell: 1).

Immigration made the modern West more or less what it is becoming: nations of migrants and cultures, especially in the urban centres, increasingly hybrid, polyglot, fluid and cosmopolitan. Michael Ignatieff in reflecting on the circumstances of his family in *The Russian Album* writes, "This century has made migration, expatriation and exile the norm, rootedness the exception. To come as I do from a hybrid family of White Russian exiles who married Scottish Canadians is to be at once lucky — we survived — and typical"

(1987: 1). It is quite right for Ignatieff to describe the evolving ethnic mix of a people as "typical," and also how with very little unrest Canada as a representative of Western liberal democracy visibly changed in these years.

I observed the change from the inside as I was part of the process that turned Canada "from a society of almost uniform colour to one that is multi-hued; from a society that was of almost uniform religion to one that is multi-faithed" (Bissoondath: 45). I arrived in Toronto a few years after the centennial year as an immigrant/refugee from war torn South Asia. I witnessed a civil war and genocide as Pakistan tore itself apart in 1971, and was lucky to escape in the midst of the killings with my mother and younger siblings from what is now Bangladesh for shelter in my grandparents' home in my native city of Calcutta, India. My parents' generation had been uprooted by the great partition of India in 1947, and within a generation my family was again thrown into the maelstrom of ethnically driven politics. The memory of the terror and savage killings that I witnessed and that nearly struck me and the male members of my family down — it is a mystery to me how we survived the rapidly changing currents of organized killings by the Pakistani military and the enraged response of mobs out for revenge — has remained vivid with me despite the passage of many years.

In Canada I found safety, support and the opportunity to begin a new life with all the promise my adopted home held forth for me. In time I came to feel uncomfortable with the notion of being a hyphenated Canadian. The part of me that belonged to the wider Indian culture I inherited at birth without any effort on my part. But the part of me, the much greater part, through the university education I acquired and the air I breathed as I mingled with the people around me at school, in work, and in politics, became by choice and conscious effort Canadian. I am a naturalized citizen of a Canada that is an integral part of the West as a civilization distinct from other civilizations and cultures. It is this awareness of choosing to be Canadian and what this implies that has grown within me since I landed in Toronto in 1974. To be Canadian in the fullest sense means, I believe, to embrace the West and freely assimilate its distinctive culture. It means to recognize, as I did with a mixture of awe and gratitude, that the West represents the idea of a civilization nurtured by the values of the Enlightenment that Kant famously defined as "dare to know," its genealogy traced back to ancient Greece, its faith tradition anchored in Judeo-Christian ethics, its politics shaped by the democratic impulse of revolutions against hereditary rule, its philosophy influenced by the development of the scientific method of controlled experiments and tests, its culture open and embracing of new ideas. The sum total of these values uniquely defines the West in terms of liberal democracy; and freedom affirms the Kantian principle that man as a free agent and a rational creature is an end in himself and must never be treated as a means to someone else's ends. My own journey from the East to the West has been an education that encourages putting aside those ideas and values that confine an individual to the requirements of collective identity and group solidarity, which Ibn Khaldun, the great Arab philosopher of the fourteenth century from North Africa, described as *asabiyya* to explain the rise and fall of political dynasties, and embracing the notions of individual liberty and freedom of conscience that Mill later most compellingly defended and that are at the foundation of politics and culture of the West.

"The struggle between liberty and authority," Mill wrote in beginning his essay *On Liberty*, "is the most conspicuous feature in the portions of history with which we are earliest familiar, particularly in that of Greece, Rome, and England" (1974: 59). This struggle is the oldest and most persistent in all of human history, and it is tilted in favour of the collective over the individual. In our time this struggle has been given a new edge by the aggressiveness of those who insist on group identity over the right of the individual to be free of any coercion that limits his freedom. Across the world, as globalization has accelerated, the collectivist demands of jihad are pushing hard against the values of liberalism. This is the return of the primitive and the denial of the view that progress in history results from the daring of the few to question the consensus of the many; it is bending to the wishes of the crowd and its unwillingness to protect the minority from the tyranny of the majority; it is the jihad of the tribe, of the class-based or ethnic-based or religiously-organized party against the ultimate minority, the solitary individual, standing alone against the weight of the many.

In this most primordial struggle between liberty and authority, the irony is that what is universal blossoms in the life of an individual as a free agent and what is particular is expressed in the dogmatic defended by the collective. Arthur Koestler's novel *Darkness at Noon* captures this essential dilemma of human existence between ends and means, between the individual's struggle for freedom of conscience and the party principle that truth is what secures and advances the collective interest. Koestler describes this conflict in a fictional setting representing Stalinist Russia to unmask the reality of totalitarian politics: "The infinite was a politically suspect quantity, the 'I' a suspect quality. The Party did not recognize its existence. The definition of the individual was: a multitude of one million divided by one million" (1964: 204). In other words, an individual is a cog in a machine and, contrary to Kant's liberal ethics, a means to an end as defined by the collective. This is the politics of jihad, which has been the normal condition for humankind in history, and only for brief tantalizing moments has the promise of liberty, as what *ought* to be the true condition for humankind, appeared on history's stage. It is in this sense that liberalism, it might be said, is a fighting creed devoted to protecting freedom as the *necessary* condition for securing human dignity against the politics of jihad.

II.

If the West has become multi-ethnic in a fit of absent-mindedness, as Christopher Caldwell has suggested, then the cure proposed and turned into an "official" policy of multiculturalism increasingly appears to have been hastily conjured out of bad faith in response to the political needs of the moment. In Canada the Trudeau initiative of October 1971 to promote multiculturalism as an official policy was merely an initiative — once we strip away the words of the prime minister delivered in Parliament — as a feel-good public pronouncement that would do no harm, an after-thought to the more urgent need to quell the nationalist fervour of the French-speaking population in Quebec. Six months later, in April 1972, Canada went to the polls, and the Liberal party under Trudeau barely managed to cling to power. For Trudeau the electoral result was a moment of catharsis, an awakening to the brutal reality that politics, as most things in life, is driven by passion, not reason. It is surprising that Trudeau as a political philosopher of some merit had not paid sufficient attention to this reality, which the Scottish philosopher David Hume (1711-76) addressed by pointing out that human action is a product of passion or desires, and that reason is at best the slave of passion, directing it once man has been moved to act.

Trudeau had entered politics with the reputation of possessing a rational intellect for cool, dispassionate, and tough analysis to handle the most delicate file in Canadian politics: the pressures on the federation as a result of the growing alienation of Quebec from English Canada. Multiculturalism as an idea was not on his mental horizon. But the 1972 election sent a tremor through him as he stared at the real likelihood of losing power, which would amount to a personal defeat in public. In an extended and privately revealing post-election interview with Patrick Watson in December 1973, Trudeau said:

I'd almost say that my faith in politics, my faith in the democratic process has changed a bit. I used to think it would be sufficient to put a reasonable proposition to a person, for the person to look at it reasonably, without passion, but that's obviously not true. Nine-tenths of politics — debate in Parliament, speeches in the hustings, commentary by the media, nine-tenths of it appeals to emotion rather than to reason. I'm a bit sorry about that, but this is the world we're living in, and therefore I've had to change (Quoted in Gwyn 1980: 138-9).

And so Trudeau emerged in the period after 1972, in the words of one of his biographers, Richard Gwyn, as a "northern magus," a leader who would relate to his party and his country by responding to the political needs of the moment, by appealing to emotions that moved people. It was out of such political calculations that the vaguely conceived multicultural initiative of 1971 was made into official policy of the government of Canada, while it became an electoral switch for the Liberal party to secure immigrant votes permanently for itself and place it at a commanding advantage in national politics over its main political rivals, the Tories and the New Democrats. "Trudeau had been criticized for ignoring the Queen; in 1973, the Queen came to Canada twice," wrote Gwyn, "a history-making precedent, with Trudeau at her side every step of the royal progress. So he had been accused of sloughing off the ethnics; up sprang a trebled multiculturalism program that functioned as a slush fund to buy ethnic votes" (1980: 139).

Politics, especially in a liberal democracy and generally under normal circumstances, occurs on the grounds where broad consensus exists among the people on most issues publicly discussed; therefore, smart politics that makes for electoral victories tends to be opportunistic. Elections are won or lost on how political leaders can exploit the passion of the moment among the voting public; but passion disallows serious contemplation of what is on offer to the public, and how any set of policies proposed by political leaders for what they are worth should be weighed by considering their unintended effects as positive or negative rather than the immediate benefits as promised.

Multiculturalism was clearly a policy on offer in the early 1970s in Canada aimed at the requirements of a political party, the Liberal party, and similarly it would be on offer by centre-left parties in other liberal democracies of the West, to capture for the long term in politics marginal votes in electoral districts of the newly arriving immigrants. It is the difference in marginal votes in closely contested electoral districts that accounts for winning or losing in elections, and by securing the ethnic-immigrant votes in the urban centres where immigrants settled on arrival, the Liberal party — as would the Democratic party in the United States, the Labour party in Britain, the Socialist and social-democratic parties in France, Germany, and other western European countries — arranged for itself an electoral advantage that its rivals would find increasingly difficult to overcome in the polls. Political opportunism set aside the consideration that multiculturalism would give sanction to group identity and political demands on the basis of what serves the collective interest of an identifiable group based on ethnicity, religion, and, later, sexual orientation in a liberal democracy that presumably stands for protecting individual rights ahead of collective rights. Multiculturalism thus was a policy born of bad faith that undermined liberal democracy by deliberately creating a wedge between new immigrants from Third World countries and the settled population that no longer viewed itself in terms of group identity as citizens, or was actively discouraged to do so, and those who did were liable to be accused of promoting "white supremacist" or racist politics. The inherent bad-faith aspect of multiculturalism in Canada was further underscored by the Citizenship

Act of 1977, which reduced the residency requirement for citizenship from five to three years.[25] With citizenship, new immigrants acquired the right to vote after living in the country for less time than the normal life of an elected majority in Parliament. The provision, in fact, smacked of rank political opportunism to secure the immigrant vote for the Liberal party.

III.

The world is naturally diverse in being multi-ethnic and multicultural. This diversity is also naturally respected as a given wherever the liberal democratic arrangement in politics is strong and institutionalized. But the moral strength of liberalism comes from its refusal to make a fetish of this diversity. The liberal vision sees above and beyond diversity in respecting individual rights, and by defending liberty on the basis of securing individual rights liberalism acknowledges that the naturally given diversity finds its best unfettered expression through the lives of individuals as free agents in history.

Official multiculturalism, however, muddies the core liberal principle that, in a conflict, however it arises, between the right of the individual to exercise his freedom of conscience and the collective demand that the individual bend to the wishes of the group, the right of the individual takes precedence over that of the group. Multiculturalism is the slippery slope that leads to the acceptance or appeasement of the politics of jihad within a liberal democracy. Until 9/11 the fundamental contradiction between multiculturalism and liberal democracy remained obscure. This was due to the inherent bad-faith politics of multiculturalism, which exploits genuine feelings of generosity toward the disadvantaged in our world and the guilt feeling that troubles the liberal conscience when confronted with the agony of others.

---

[25] The legislation passed by the Trudeau Liberals, was long required, since Canadian citizenship until then had been an undefined category, and technically Canadians were by statute native-born or naturalized British subjects: see Young (1998).

Multiculturalists disarm and seduce liberals with the argument that "we" are responsible for the "other," that the advantages the West enjoys come at the expense of those who are disadvantaged in the less-developed non-European countries that were once colonies and dependencies of the European colonial powers. This reading of history suggests the West is culpable for the wrongs done to the people of the Third World and their cultures, and even though those wrongs cannot be entirely undone, the West can begin to meet its responsibility to make amends for those wrongs by recognizing this history. Paradoxically, however, this recognition of past wrongs by the West absolves Third World people and cultures of their own responsibility in history; it tells them that their disadvantages relative to the West are mostly, if not entirely, the result of colonial exploitations by the European powers, and that their historical progress in keeping with their own cultural values was denied them as a result of the West's colonial-imperial aggression against them.

Guilt feeling can be cathartic for individuals and societies jolted by the information and images of the inequalities in the world and by the sheer absurdity of the overabundance of commodities available to the people in the West. French writer Pascal Bruckner discussed what this means:

These images clearly describe the failures of our age. Their horror leaves no place for hope. Rather than broadening human possibilities, the dying hundreds of thousands in the Southern hemisphere defy the plans of others with their endless agony, deflating the values we hold dearest, ridiculing the greatest scientific and artistic achievements of the international community. We feel that our moral faith in mankind will not recover from this wound. And, because every day the media give the human race the knowledge of its own misfortune, an apocalyptic vision of the universe begins to spread. By setting forth daily the balance sheet of suffering around the globe, radio and television networks give our planet a terrible image — that it is unquestionably the worst of all possible worlds (1986: 44-5).

The liberal mind is readily disposed to see injustice when confronted with such disparity, and in becoming riddled with shame over that portion of history in which Europeans ruled over the non-Europeans for their own benefit, the liberal mind seeks atonement. The problems of the world are, however, immense, and the thought of finding solutions can also lead to a paralysis of the individual will to act. Governments can do better, and Western governments have been driven by a complex of reasons such as prudence, self-interest, and compassion, and prodded by liberal guilt feeling to provide economic, technological and other sorts of assistance to Third World countries. But to what extent such assistance has helped developing countries is another matter — some economists have raised serious doubts about the contribution of foreign aid to economic growth in the Third World (see, for example, Easterly, 2006; Moyo, 2009). The generosity of the West has been substantial: over the past 50 years, according to the World Bank, US $2.3 trillion has gone from advanced industrial economies to the developing countries of Asia, Africa and South America (Easterly: 4). While the West has shared its own developmental experience, it is reluctant to provide any critical assessment of how the prevailing cultures in Third World countries might be holding them back. The past weighs heavily on the liberal mind, and the resulting guilt forbids any suggestion that might undermine the multiculturalist doctrine that all cultures are essentially of equal merit and deserving of equal respect. This is the conundrum that silences liberals who are otherwise open to reasoning and analytical judgment. The multiculturalist thus wins the argument by default.

The Islamist assault on the liberal West, however, has exposed the hollowness of multiculturalism as an official policy of Western governments and the mainstream political parties that refuse to question it. The overt assault in the form of terrorism can be effectively dealt with by appropriate security measures, but it is the covert attempt to undermine liberal democracies from within by infiltrating their institutions that poses the more serious long-term Islamist threat. Like dope addicts, however, Western governments and the ideologues of multiculturalism insist that the answer to defusing the Islamist jihad by stealth is more multiculturalism, including appeasement by incrementally conceding to Islamist demands to accept *shari'ah* as a parallel legal norm for Muslim populations in the West alongside the rule of law that is secular and based on the hard-won principle of the separation of church and state.

It is because of their self-imposed inhibition that liberals in the West will not publicly state the obvious — that *shari'ah* is incompatible with the workings of the modern world. But no such inhibition constrains modern liberal Muslims. They recognize, as the modern scholarship of Islam and Muslim history illustrates, that "the classical theory of Shari'a law was the outcome of a complex historical process spanning a period of some three centuries," that "the growth of Islamic law was linked to the current social, political and economic conditions," and that this "classical exposition represents the zenith of a process whereby the specific terms of the law came to be expressed as the irrevocable will of God" (Coulson: 4). In other words, while traditionalist-minded Muslims and Islamists insist that *shari'ah* is the divine ordinance, irrevocably complete and "embodying norms of an absolute and eternal validity, which are not susceptible to modification by any legislative authority" (ibid), modern liberal Muslims see *shari'ah* as a human effort to construct a religion-based (Islamic) legal system from the piecemeal nature of pronouncements taken as legislative decrees found in the Qur'an that were in keeping with the cultural norms of the time and place when this effort was formally initiated and closed between the first century (seventh century C.E.) and the third century of Islam (tenth century C.E.). S*hari'ah*, therefore, in the view of liberal-minded Muslims, is contextually bound to the value system of the ancient and medieval world. This is how Mohamed Charfi, professor emeritus in the law faculty in Tunis and a former minister of education in Tunisia, in *Islam and Liberty: The Historical Misunderstanding* describes *shari'ah*:

Muslim law is based on three fundamental inequalities: the superiority of men over women, of Muslims over non-Muslims, and of free persons over slaves. It recognizes the maximum advantages in the case of a free and rich Muslim male, and the fewest rights in the case of a non-Muslim female slave.... Muslim law is therefore fundamentally discriminatory. It might be said that this is a harsh judgment. Indeed it is — an unfair judgment even. But what makes it necessary, unfortunately, is the existence of a fundamentalist movement that demands a return to the sharia and therefore compels us to measure the past by the standards of the present. An objective evaluation would require us to place Muslim law in its historical context and to compare it with the legal systems of other old civilizations. It then takes on a rather different aspect (2005: 78-9).

It is likely true that in the post-9/11 world of Islamist rage most Muslims, especially those who have seriously considered such matters, might not defend publicly Professor Charfi's view. But it is another matter when non-Muslims in the West shun or deny the view Professor Charfi expresses and when such a view is at the heart of the struggle for reform of Islam among Muslims. When political leaders and public figures in the West openly engage in discussing how to make room for *shari'ah* based provisions in liberal democratic societies, then undeniably such discussions are evidence of appeasement of Islamists-in-the-making disguised as multiculturalism.

In giving the foundation lecture in February 2008 at the Royal Courts of Justice in London, Archbishop of Canterbury Dr. Rowan Williams raised the likelihood that Britain might need to consider the partial adoption of *shari'ah*. The main concern he expressed was around the issue of how civil and religious law should be reconciled in a manner that preserves the rule of law while accommodating different religious norms that reflect the pluralist nature of a modern multi-ethnic and multi-faith society. He suggested that "we have to think a little harder about the role and rule of law in a plural society of overlapping identities" and he offered the view that "[i]t would be a pity if the immense advances in the recognition of human rights led, because of a misconception about legal universality, to a situation where a person was defined primarily as the possessor of a set of abstract liberties and the law's function was accordingly seen as nothing but the securing of those liberties *irrespective of the custom and conscience of those groups which concretely compose a plural modern society*" (Archbishop's Lecture 2008; italics added).

The archbishop's remarks ignited a fury of discussions in the British media over whether or not he had called for the adoption of *shari'ah*. His predecessor, Lord George Carey, responded that the archbishop had "overstated the case for accommodating Islamic legal codes. His conclusion that Britain will eventually have to concede some place in law for aspects of sharia is a view I cannot share."[26] The context for the controversy was the militancy of a growing portion of the Muslim immigrant population in Britain and Islamist attacks carried out in that country, as well as the appearance of *shari'ah*

---

[26] Quoted in R. Butt, "Gordon Brown backs archbishop in sharia law row," *Guardian*, February 11, 2008.

tribunals within the wider Islamic community in Britain dealing with family disputes, marriages, divorces, child custody, inheritance and property rights. One US critic of the archbishop and the Anglican hierarchy observed, "The problem, shared by much of the Anglican establishment, is a culture of political correctness that is at once too generous and too stingy: an eagerness to overlook the staggering problems in Islamic thought with regard to democratic rights, but a reluctance to claim any decisive role for biblical religion in the formation and defense of those rights."[27] But the archbishop's remarks on *shari'ah* were in keeping with the goals of multiculturalism to accommodate in the politics and law of a liberal democracy the group-based identities of people belonging to immigrant communities, and to accept the cultural norms by which these communities live. Such recognition also would be consistent, he suggested, with the expansive meaning of human rights that had evolved in a liberal society such as Britain.

A similar effort was made in Ontario by a former attorney-general, Marion Boyd, with the release of a report in December 2004 counselling the Liberal government of Premier Dalton McGuinty to adopt provisions of *shari'ah* for the purpose of arbitration in family and inheritance matters. McGuinty declined to accept Boyd's recommendation given the public unease with the post-9/11 reality, yet the push for recognition of *shari'ah* in a Canadian jurisdiction remains a priority for Islamists in Canada. According to a Muslim activist-lawyer in Ontario,

Boyd's report merely affirms *our* Constitutional right to religious freedom, equal treatment under the law, [and] multiculturalism and ensures that we are in compliance with our international obligations. Indeed, Article 27 of the *International Covenant on Civil and Political Rights*, to which Canada acceded on May 19, 1976, imposes a positive duty on a state to assist its minorities to preserve its [sic] values by allowing them to enjoy their own culture and to profess and practise their own religion.[28]

---

[27] J. Loconte, "Allah, Queen, and Country: Sharia gets an unlikely boost in the UK," *The Weekly Standard*, February 13, 2008.
[28] F. Kutty, "Boyd's recommendations balance needs of religious communities with rights of vulnerable," *The Lawyers Weekly* (Toronto), January 21, 2005.

It is the vulnerability of liberal democracies that the tools by which liberals have advanced the principles of individual rights and secured them in law are equally available, and often provided by liberals themselves, to those who either do not believe in such principles or subordinate them to collective rights on the basis provided for, as Kutty claims in making his case for recognition of *shari'ah* provisions, by multiculturalism and international covenants on human rights. This is not simply a matter of bad faith, of liberalism turned on its head to tear down the historical characteristics of a liberal democracy, such as Britain. It is ridiculous, and of this sort of absurdity one critic of multiculturalism, in reference to a political philosopher of Indian origin made life peer in 2000 by Prime Minister Tony Blair to secure ethnic Indian votes for his Labour Party, wrote as follows: "One professor of race relations, Bikhu Parekh, has even suggested that Britain should change its name, which has so many negative historical connotations for millions around the world. Now that Britain has become so ineradicably multicultural, he says, there is no justification for it to be 'British' any more" (Dalrymple: 216).

This vulnerability was acute during the Cold War years, when the internal enemies of liberal democracy on the left (communists) and on the right (fascists) made claims for their right to espouse anti-democratic views on the basis of liberal values. As the French political philosopher Jean-François Revel remarked, "Democratic civilization is the first in history to blame itself because another power is working to destroy it...What distinguishes it is its eagerness to believe in its own guilt and...is zealous in devising arguments to prove the justice of its adversary's case and to lengthen the already overwhelming list of its own inadequacies" (Revel: 7-8).

In the post-9/11 world, guilt feeling in the West has been debased into political correctness that frowns on any critical inquiry into the validity of the general assumptions of multiculturalism. Political correctness comes wearing the garment of anthropologists whose training in studying the minute details of different cultures and faithfully rendering them — as Clifford Geertz, a distinguished member of the discipline, calls for — through "thick description" prevents them from assessing cultures on the basis of some objective and independent standard (Geertz, 1973: chap. 1). Cultures are inherently different from one another, but the important question is not how cultures differ but what do such differences indicate in terms of their past achievements and current ability to contribute to the advancement of our increasingly shared history. Since such a question invariably points to the objective reality that all cultures are not equal in terms of either past achievements or current viability according to some agreed independent standard of measurement, political correctness forbids asking it. Instead, multiculturalism promotes the notion of cultural relativism, which states that since each culture is by definition unique, any independent standard to distinguish among cultures would itself represent cultural bias nullifying the objectivity of any test applied. The syllogism of the proponents of multiculturalism is therefore a closed loop where differences among cultures amount to the proof that all cultures are equal, and the questioning of this syllogism then indicates racism — the dreadful "R" word, the scarlet letter in the politically correct world of multiculturalism that disarms liberals and prevents critical thought.

Moreover, the claim that cultural relativism reflects an openness of mind to connect with and learn about other cultures paradoxically has the opposite effect — that this politically correct openness is shallow in the absence or prohibition of critical thinking on matters related to cultures. Allan Bloom discussed this paradox in *The Closing of the American Mind* as follows:

Men cannot remain content with what is given them by their culture if they are to be fully human. This is what Plato meant to show by the image of the cave in the *Republic* and by representing us as prisoners in it. A culture is a cave. He did not suggest going around to other cultures as a solution to the limitations of the cave. Nature should be the standard by which we judge our own lives and the lives of people. That is why philosophy, not history or anthropology, is the most important human science. Only dogmatic assurance that thought is culture-bound, that there is no nature, is what makes our educators so certain that the only way to escape the limitations of our time and place is to study other cultures.

This point of view, particularly the need to know nature in order to have a standard, is uncomfortably buried beneath our human sciences, whether they like it or not, and accounts for the ambiguities and contradictions I have been pointing out. They want to make us culture-beings with the instruments that were invented to liberate us from culture. *Openness used to be the virtue that permitted us to seek the good by using reason. It now means accepting everything and denying reason's power.* The unrestrained and thoughtless pursuit of openness, without recognizing the inherent political, social, or cultural problem of openness as the goal of nature, has rendered openness meaningless. *Cultural relativism destroys both one's own and the good.* What is most characteristic of the West is science, particularly understood as the quest to know nature and the consequent denigration of convention — i.e., culture or the West understood as a culture — in favor of what is accessible to all men as men through their common and distinctive faculty, reason. Science's latest attempts to grasp the human situation — cultural relativism, historicism, the fact-value distinction — are the suicide of science. *Culture, hence closedness, reigns supreme. Openness to closedness is what we teach* (1987: 38-9; italics added).

In the post-9/11 world, the indiscriminate openness of cultural relativism that leads to tolerating the politics of jihad reveals the absurdity of multiculturalism. Political correctness in such circumstances is a death wish by denying our critical faculty, the mind, through reasoning to discriminate among things, circumstances, opinions, dogmas, people, institutions, and so on in liberating us from superstition and from the closed circle of tribal politics.

IV.

The politics of multiculturalism works in tandem with the politics of immigration. A generation after the immigration reforms of the 1960s — whether resulting from the rising liberal optimism about the future, as the West repaired the terrible wounds of the Second World War, or from the tumbling birth rates and the need for workers in low-end jobs — the population of the West has undergone a visibly changed ethnic profile. By the 2001 census, 18.4 percent of Canada's population was born outside the country; in Australia, the foreign-born accounted for 22 percent of the population (Statistics Canada 2003: 5). But any critical examination of immigration policy in Canada, as in the rest of the West, is taboo due to the politics of multiculturalism. There is a public consensus that Canada as a country of immigrants should be welcoming of immigrants, as they contribute to its economic well-being and are an answer to the problem of an aging population. This is a view that no one in politics or the mainstream media is willing to question or examine objectively.

There was a time, however, between the end of World War II and the immigration reforms of the 1960s when immigration into Canada, as in most countries of the West, was controlled on the basis of prevalent economic conditions. This changed in the 1970s and 1980s, as James Bissett, a retired Canadian diplomat and senior public servant in Ottawa, explains. Once immigration was politicized, all political parties sought electoral advantage by supporting open immigration with higher numbers of immigrants granted entry. According to Bissett,

[in] 1985 the newly elected Progressive Conservative government of Prime Minister Brian Mulroney raised immigration levels despite evidence of an economic down-turn. This was the signal that the Conservative party was determined to win ethnic votes by supporting high immigration levels. In 1990, the then Minister, Barbara McDougal, convinced her cabinet colleagues to raise the levels to 250,000, by arguing that higher levels would help the party to establish stronger ties with ethnic communities. Later, the Minister said in an interview that a political party was not doing its job if it failed to reach out to ethnic groups. There was political capital to be gained by high numbers whether they were needed or not (2009: 4).

Since the immigration tap, once opened, creates its own pressures that will not allow for it to be closed easily, making the West more multi-ethnic and multi-faith likely will remain irreversible. This fact should not necessarily be a cause for alarm, except for the reality of the post-9/11 situation.

Since 9/11 the Muslim population in the West has not shown forthrightness and determination in repudiating Islamism as an ideology that increasingly makes a mockery of Islam as a peaceful religion tolerant of other faith-traditions or in isolating the Islamists. In Europe, in particular, there is concern about what the growth of Muslim immigrants means for the continent's culture and for liberal democracy. Muslims in Europe are now estimated to number in around 38 million, or about 5 per cent of the population. As Caldwell writes, "In the middle of the twentieth century, there were virtually no Muslims in Western Europe. At the turn of the twenty-first century, there were between 15 and 17 million Muslims" (2009: 12). In contrast, Muslims account for less than 1 percent of the total population of Canada and the United States (Pew 2009a: 32-3). These numbers will increase relatively quickly through immigration, especially under the family re-unification policy, and a higher fertility rate within the Muslim immigrant communities than among the native non-Muslim population. It is the meaning of these numbers projected into the future that raises alarm, especially among those Europeans who fear their culture is being undermined by the twin forces of immigration and multiculturalism.

The European dilemma as a cautionary note for North America is in how its liberal democratic culture is becoming increasingly relativistic by adopting the politics of multiculturalism and contending with immigrant cultures, particularly that of Muslims, confident of their values. There is the easy conflict-avoidance path of appeasement based on the hope that the more Europe accommodates Islam, the more Muslims will respond by respecting European values and resisting demands that make a mockery of European liberalism. Islamists, however, are not ideologically motivated to seek coexistence on terms set by others; for them, coexistence means setting the terms for others on the basis of *shari'ah* values that are incompatible with liberal values. In the end, the European dilemma means, as Caldwell summarizes, "[w]hen an insecure, malleable, relativistic culture meets a culture that is anchored, confident, and strengthened by common doctrines, it is generally the former that changes to suit the latter" (2009: 349). A Europe turned into a "Eurabia" then would be the legacy of immigration joined with multiculturalism as official policy that tolerates the intolerant and lethally undermines a civilization from the inside. Or in the words of Arnold Toynbee, the historian of civilizations, as Mark Steyn reminds us, "Civilizations die from suicide, not murder."[29]

The paradox of multiculturalism was unavoidable and predictable once a liberal democracy, such as Canada, willingly embraced an idea that was a concoction of loose thinking and bad faith. It also turned out to be a sort of soft bigotry — "a racism of the anti-racists: it chains people to their roots"[30] — disguised as the high-minded virtue of being open to diversity and respecting differences among cultures but that amounted to viewing immigrants from the

---

[29] M. Steyn, "It's the Demography, Stupid," *The New Criterion*, January 2006.
[30] P. Bruckner, "Enlightenment fundamentalism or racism of the anti-racists?" *signandsight.com*, January 24, 2007.

Third World not as individuals but as people confined within the particulars of their birth cultures. This meant that such immigrants were neither expected nor asked to make the passage from their traditional cultures and embrace modernity with its liberal values. This is also the paradox of multiculturalism, according to Bruckner, as "it accords the same treatment to all communities, but not to the people who form them, denying them the freedom to liberate themselves from their own traditions. Instead: recognition of the group, oppression of the individual" (ibid). In celebrating diversity on the basis of cultural relativism and pushing political correctness, multiculturalism has done its share to weaken the confidence of the West in its own cultural inheritance by undermining critical thinking about cultures when most needed to push back the politics of global jihad.

Chapter Eight

SUMMING UP

In an April 23, 2010, newspaper column, Ujjal Dosanjh, former premier of British Columbia and at the time Member of Parliament for Vancouver South, called on Canadians to ask the tough questions: "What will Canada look like in 50 years? Will we still have a country that is fair, compassionate, just, integrated and socially cohesive, bound by fundamental core values? Or will we live separately, in communities that are islands unto themselves? Could there be separatist voices rising from communities in Canada, so extreme and so violent that we may long for the days of the peaceful advocacy of the Parti Québécois and Bloc Québécois?"[31] Dosanjh's words carried the weight of his own harrowing personal experiences as a victim of political violence. He had been physically beaten, and was fortunate to escape with his life, for publicly opposing extremists in the Sikh community to which he belongs. In his column, Dosanjh contends, that minority communities — that is, mostly those of non-European origin — by being "obsessively focused on injustices" in their native countries and thereby importing quarrels from distant lands, threatened social harmony within Canada.

It was the obsessive focus on injustices faced by Sikhs in India — irrespective of the fact that the Sikh community is one of the most successful minority groups in the Hindu-majority country and, as I write, Manmohan Singh, the prime minister of India, happens to be a

---

[31] Ujjal Dosanjh, "Ask the tough questions," *National Post*, April 23, 2010.

Sikh — that led Sikh extremists in Canada to plan and execute the worst terrorist act before 9/11 when they blew up an Air India plane, killing all passengers on a flight from Toronto to New Delhi in June 1985. Similarly, conflicts in the Middle East, in South Asia, in Africa, and elsewhere have generated tensions among ethnic minorities in Canada, Europe, the United States, and Australia. The effect of such politics, as Dosanjh notes, brings increasing stress on tolerance· in a society with a rapidly changing demography, as is Canada. This unpleasant fact was discussed in a cover story by *Maclean's* magazine.[32]

The *Maclean's* story reported Canadian views about religion and faith-based identity found in a national survey of public opinion. The findings were disturbing for a country that has made multiculturalism its credo. The report indicated that 72 percent of Canadians thought favourably of Christianity, while only 28 percent viewed Islam favourably and 30 percent viewed Sikhism positively (the figures for Hinduism, Buddhism and Judaism were, respectively, 41 percent, 57 percent and 53 percent). When asked how far governments should go to accommodate minorities, 62 percent agreed with the statement "Laws and norms should not be modified to accommodate minorities." In Quebec, "74 per cent were against changing laws or norms, the highest negative response rate on the accommodation question in the country." Divisiveness within Canada emanating from cultural differences as the *Maclean's* poll revealed, was a surprise for those Canadians who had convinced themselves of the virtue of multiculturalism and that it made their country "a model for the world of how all sorts of people can get along together."

Multiculturalism is based on the premise that, because the world is culturally diverse, this diversity needs to be acknowledged and promoted as public policy within liberal democracies, since these societies as a result of immigration increasingly reflect that diversity within their respective state boundaries. As Bhikhu Parekh notes, the multiculturalist perspective takes into consideration "the cultural embeddedness of human beings, the inescapability and desirability of cultural plurality, and the plural and multicultural constitution of each

---

[32] "What Canadians think of Sikhs, Jews, Christians, Muslims…" *Maclean's*, May 4, 2009.

culture."[33] But exponents of multiculturalism ignore, or deliberately set aside, the unique nature of the culture that evolved in the West and flourishes in the liberal democracies of Europe and North America, the progeny of the Enlightenment that fundamentally altered man's conception of God and nature and his relationship to both. The modern West shaped by the Enlightenment did not repudiate religion, but instead subjected religion to the scrutiny of reason. The result was the making of the secular conscience based on the universality of reason in contrast to religious conscience based on the dictates of religion and the authority of the church (Dacey: 8-22). Secularism, as the conservative philosopher Roger Scruton explains, is a sort of religious belief and duty where worship of an abstract God is a private affair and tolerance of religious and other differences is the cardinal virtue. He writes:

Voltaire and the Encyclopedists, Hume, Smith, and the Scottish Enlightenment, the Kant of *Religion within the Limits of Reason Alone* — such thinkers and movements had collectively remade the God of Christianity as a creature of the head rather than the heart. God retreated from the world to the far reaches of infinite space, where only vertiginous thoughts could capture him. Daily life is of little concern to such a God, who demands no form of obedience except to the universal precepts of morality. To worship him is to bow in private towards the unknowable (2002: 43).

Thus, the unique transmutation of Western culture and civilization brought about by the Enlightenment and the new scientific method pioneered by Galileo led to the separation of church and state, religion and politics, and a new form of association and membership or belonging — that is, one of citizenship — within the state. Membership is the prerequisite of every society, giving an identity to the individuals who belong to it; in this sense, such an identity is pre-political, and the culture it produces becomes instrumental in the making of political institutions and politics of that society. Again Scruton:

---

[33] B. Parekh, "What is multiculturalism?" *Seminar* (web-edition), New Delhi, December 1999; available online at www.india-seminar.com.

Membership is defined in different ways at different times and places. For many societies, religion is an important part of it, so that the infidel is cast out or marginalized, as in traditional Islamic society. Although religion has been an important part of European identity, it was gradually, under the influence of the Enlightenment, pushed into the background by nationality, and subsequently by the rise of the nation state. And it is thanks to the nation state that we enjoy the freedoms and secular jurisdictions that are so attractive to immigrants — and especially to those immigrants who define their pre-political membership in religious, rather than national, terms. For national loyalty is a form of neighbourliness: it is loyalty to a shared home and to the people who have built it. It makes no specific demands of a religious or ideological nature, and is content with a common obedience to a secular rule of the law, and a common sense of belonging to the land, its customs and its habits of peaceful coexistence. Communities founded on a national rather than a religious conception of membership are *inherently open* to newcomers, in the way that religious communities are not. An immigrant to a religious community must be prepared to convert; an immigrant to a national community need only obey the law.[34]

The notion of citizenship is what brings people together in a liberal democracy and binds them in a relationship of mutual obligations. The sense of belonging as a result of membership in a modern state is qualitatively different than one in a tribe, a family, or a club, since the obligations that come with membership, are to strangers with whom an individual shares in common the association of belonging to that state. Citizenship is the identity by which an individual claims he has a country to call his own and shares in its sovereignty (Dunn 2005: 117). A citizen, one writer notes, is "someone who possesses rights which are denied in a legally stratified or segmented society to non-citizens and in all societies to resident aliens and foreigners" (Heater: 247). In his judgment in *Perez v. Brownell* (1958), U.S. Chief Justice Earl Warren wrote, "Citizenship *is* man's basic right for it is nothing less than the right to have rights. Remove this priceless possession and there remains a stateless person, disgraced and degraded in the eyes of his countrymen" (quoted in Heater; italics in original).

---

[34] R. Scruton, "Immigration, Multiculturalism and the Need to Defend the Nation State," *The Brussels Journal* June 24, 2006 (italics added); available online www.brusselsjournal.com/node/1126.

But this idea of citizenship is modern and secular. It is the fruit of the Western civic culture, and while other cultures have borrowed this idea, it is only in the West that citizenship is vested in a free individual with rights and responsibilities. The animating spirit of a free individual as citizen is the loyalties he shares in common with others to the territorially demarcated state to which he belongs, to the liberal democratic or republican constitution of that state which he is sworn to uphold and defend, and to the laws of the state in whose sovereignty he has a share. And the identity provided by citizenship in a modern liberal democratic state takes precedence over all other identities, those of the political left and right or of overlapping ethnic, religious, cultural, and professional identities that proliferate in an open society.

Multiculturalism, however, works to weaken or dissolve citizenship identity by suggesting that the cultural identities which immigrants bring with them deserve to be recognized and treated with equal respect. As I have indicated, tolerance is the virtue esteemed in liberal democracy and its inherent characteristic is acceptance of other cultures. But this acceptance cannot mean a denial of its own historically evolved civic culture represented by the modern and secular idea of citizenship. The problem arises and persists when multiculturalism demands that liberal democracy recognize in law cultural practices that are not merely different, but contrary and oppositional to its core values of citizenship rights and responsibilities, individual freedom, and democracy. Any concession to group-based identity — for instance, recognizing in law the status of women in accordance with Islamic practice based on *shari'ah* — would undermine the principle of gender equality in a liberal democracy.

Increasingly multiculturalism, in espousing acceptance of other cultures, irrespective of how such acceptance diminishes liberal democracy's unique set of values — most importantly the place of the individual citizen as a minority of one protected by the full panoply of the state's power based on the rule of law — has turned out to be an insidious assault on freedom in the West. This espousal by proponents of multiculturalism is motivated in part from a sense of both generosity given the immensity of capitalist wealth, and guilt of the West's history of colonialism and imperialism; it is also motivated by a loss of faith in the legacy of the Enlightenment and opposition to the idea of the nation-state as it originated and evolved in the West.

There are enemies of the West who hate its civic culture, its freedom and democracy, as do the Islamists who organized the terrorist strikes on 9/11. And ironically these enemies find that multiculturalism increasingly in the post-9/11 world works in tandem with their interests to weaken the West politically and culturally from the inside. The reason multiculturalism gives comfort to the enemies of the West is explained, Robert Fulford says, by lack of self-confidence: "Since the success of Martin Luther in the sixteenth century, the West has revered self-criticism. We all know that the states in North and South America established themselves by violence and that Europe grew rich through its colonies. In the universities the young learn one central belief: We are guilty! In comparing ourselves with other forms of society, our first self-hating instinct is to adopt a perverse moral disarmament."[35] This self-hating instinct, Pascal Bruckner reminds us, is also uniquely Western. "Europe against itself: anti-Occidentalism, as we know," he writes, "is a European tradition that stretches from Montaigne to Sartre and instills relativism and doubt in a serene conscience sure that it is right" (2010: 9). Whatever once were the good intentions behind multiculturalism, it has become, in the post-9/11 world as a post-modern ideology, the tool of "guilt peddlers" — Bruckner's apt description of those who reflexively fault the West for most, if not all, of the world's problems — to tear down the West.

II.

Multiculturalism as public policy in Canada and in other liberal democracies is not likely to be disowned and dismantled by governments in the immediate future. It has acquired a momentum of its own, and those who have invested in propagating it since the early 1970s have succeeded in entrenching it within all the major institutions of the country. Hence multiculturalism as a doctrine, much like the socialist creed, is resistant to the test of falsification: no matter how compelling is the contrary evidence to the claims of

---

[35] R. Fulford, "The West has work to do," *National Post*, December 26, 2009.

multiculturalism, no matter how insidiously it corrupts the core values of liberal democracy, there is the "progressive" appeal for social justice derived from the notion of equality ahead of liberty, and adorned in a contrite language pushing for reform as atonement for past wrongs, that makes multiculturalism an attractive notion to many members of an open society.

The best that might be done under these circumstances to oppose the ideology of multiculturalism, and to seek its eventual repudiation both in the realm of ideas and in legislation, is to contain its further spread into the workings of liberal democracy. The rise and spread of militant Islamism with the success of the Islamic revolution in Iran — ironically, this movement coincided with the push for adoption of multiculturalism as public policy in Canada — and its combativeness against the West poses the most serious challenge to the proponents and defenders of multiculturalism in government, in schools and institutions of higher learning, in the media, and in mainstream political parties. This Islamist assault on the West provides the opening to question the basis of multiculturalism and to contain its further spread.

Since 9/11 there has been a growing sense of alarm in the West among people at large that their open, tolerant society and its unique civic culture are under siege by their own governments, which are seen as excessively sensitive to the cultural needs of new immigrants instead of defending their ways of living. In Quebec, residents of Hérouxville, a small township outside of Montreal, brought this alarm to a head when they published a charter that called for anyone moving into their township to abide by its terms. The Hérouxville charter resonated among the majority population of French-Canadians in Quebec, and in order to be seen as a responsive government, Quebec's Liberal premier Jean Charest set up the Bouchard-Taylor Commission to look into the grievances and come forward with recommendations. The commission's report, released in 2008, called for "reasonable accommodation" between the native-born population and the growing numbers of newly arriving immigrants from non-European cultures. The commissioners conceded, "Our society is sufficiently divided at present and we must seek to reduce splits and tensions instead of exacerbating them. The time has come for compromise, negotiation and balance" (Bouchard and Taylor: 10).

Yet the dilemma with "reasonable accommodation" is how the majority population can insist that new immigrants adopt the civic culture of liberal democracy when government-approved multiculturalism rejects the need for assimilation in favour of extending equal recognition to other cultures. This contradiction was exposed in the controversy surrounding the subject of the *niqab* — the practice by some Muslim women of fully covering of their body and face except for the eyes — when Quebec immigration minister Yolande James approved the expulsion from class in a Montreal school of a student, an Egyptian woman, for refusing to bare her face and insisting that male students in the class refrain from facing her. In the weeks following this incident Premier Charest introduced Bill 94 in Quebec's National Assembly in March 2010 requiring anyone employed by the government and publicly funded institutions — Crown corporations, hospitals, schools, universities, daycare centres, libraries, and other municipal facilities — or receiving their services to uncover their face for the purposes of identification. For multiculturalists, Bill 94 is a violation of the rights of minorities to maintain their respective cultural precepts, and if the bill becomes law it is very likely it will be taken to the human rights commissions in both Quebec and Ottawa and appealed in the courts.

Quebec is not alone in demanding that Muslim women unveil in public — the issue has become even more volatile in Europe. The linguistically divided Belgian parliament voted overwhelmingly to ban face covering in April 2010, setting a precedent for France and now possibly the Netherlands to follow. Jean-François Copé, the majority leader in the French National Assembly and the mayor of Meaux, explained, "This is not an article of clothing — it is a mask, a mask worn at all times, making identification or participation in economic and social life virtually impossible." In anticipating opposition similar to the condemnation by Amnesty International of the Belgian ban as "an attack on religious freedom," he then continued,

in both France and the United States, we recognize that individual liberties cannot exist without individual responsibilities. This acknowledgment is the basis of all our political rights. We are free as long as we are responsible individuals who can be held accountable for our actions before our peers. But the niqab and burka represent a refusal to exist as a person in the eyes of others. The person who wears one is no longer identifiable; she is a shadow among others, lacking individuality, avoiding responsibility.[36]

It is quite proper that people in liberal democracies and their representatives in government remain wary about defending individual rights and freedoms without breaching the same of others in society. The *niqab* controversy illustrates, however, the difficulties when the principle of citizenship is set aside or not given precedence over cultural norms as basis of identity that are inconsistent with modern secular values.

In resisting the corrosive effects of multiculturalism on a liberal democracy, the principle of citizenship with its rights and responsibilities needs to be reaffirmed and protected. People need to be reminded repeatedly what it means to be a citizen in a modern secular state, and why any form of multicultural citizenship or dual and multiple citizenship that most liberal democracies, including Canada, have adopted in practice is a contradiction in terms, weakening and diminishing the identity of citizens who are joined together in commonly shared loyalty to their state. In his usual trenchant style, George Jonas dissects this contradiction as follows:

I'm often called a Hungarian-Canadian. It doesn't bother me, but it's inaccurate. I'd only be a Hungarian-Canadian if I were a citizen of both countries, and I'm not.

I was born and raised in Hungary, survived it and when an alternative opened up, I became a Canadian. That was about half a century ago. I've been a Canadian ever since. Not a Hungarian-Canadian, but a Canadian....

A person may derive his or her identity from many things, including occupation, sex, race, religion, class, nationality and citizenship. Not all identities are exclusive. Some can obviously overlap or may even be complementary....

Other identities are exclusive. They cannot be hyphenated. If you are, or choose to be one thing, by definition you cannot be the other. It would be difficult to describe a person as a "Canadian woman-man" (even if you think someone you know fits the definition). What about hermaphrodites, someone may ask. Well, what about them? They have a category of their own.

---

[36] J.-F. Copé, "Tearing away the veil," *New York Times*, May 4, 2010.

The point is, there are identities that don't exist in multiples. Genders, citizenships, marital statuses, and the like cannot be stacked without altering their essence....

A citizen is a spouse. He or she can be attracted to several countries, but married to only one. There are Turks living in Denmark, and Danes with memories of Turkey, but no Danish Turks. I've many memories of Hungary, including some fond ones, and feel enriched by knowing something of its language, literature, music, customs and geography, but find patriotism as indivisible as Solomon's baby. My reservoir of patriotic feelings is exhausted by Canada, and citizenship without patriotic feelings is a sham.

Dual citizenship appears to me a loveless marriage, a marriage of convenience. I've fond memories of previous wives and know something of their geography and music, but my current wife exhausts my reservoir of spousal feelings. She's entitled to my unhyphenated commitment. So is my country.[37]

Jonas is certainly not alone in his patriotic sentiment, in his affection for and singular loyalty to his country that comes with an awareness of the meaning of citizenship. My sentiments are similar to those of Jonas, and it would be with most people who value their citizenship, whether they are native born or naturalized. These sentiments are in the best sense deeply felt and nurtured, are as natural as is familial affection or love between two people and not merely some sort of convention, utilitarian, artificially rigged, and bureaucratically supervised. But dual and multiple citizenships make a mockery of patriotic sentiments and reduce the principle of citizenship with its rights and obligations to a matter of convenience. Together with multiculturalism, dual and multiple citizenships work to hollow out the modern secular state and turn it into an attractive hotel, a comfortable and convenient way station for people on the move in the age of mass migration, of globalization of finance and commerce, and of rapid transportation and instant communication. As a result, however, whatever gains or profits are declared in the audited annual reports of national treasuries and multinational corporations, the incremental loss of individual freedom in a liberal democracy over time becomes irreversible and the future of open society becomes increasingly bleak.

---

[37] G. Jonas, "Dual citizenship: A contradiction in terms," *National Post*, June 9, 2010.

III.

In March 2010 a rare and unusual debate took place in the Senate, or the upper house, of the Canadian parliament. The subject of the debate was on a motion moved by the Conservative Senator Doug Finley, the "Erosion of Freedom of Speech." In his remarks, Finley urged his fellow Senators consider the extent to which free speech in Canada was under siege from officially appointed censors in the human rights commissions, in the media, in the universities, and those self-appointed who could mobilize a mob to shut down speech they disapproved. He reminded his peers that Canada inherited the tradition of free speech from Great Britain and France, and that it "is as Canadian as maple syrup, hockey and the northern lights" (Hansard, 2010). But then Finley said:

Yet, despite our 400-year tradition of free speech, the tyrannical instinct to censor still exists. We saw it on a university campus last week, and we see it every week in Canada's misleadingly named human rights commissions (Ibid).

The reference to university was the University of Ottawa's cancellation of a speaking event for Ann Coulter, a right-wing American political commentator and author, due to fears that student demonstrations against her views might incite violence. But the odd thing in this decision was even before Ms. Coulter would have spoken, she was cautioned in a letter by François Houle, the university's vice-president, that promoting "hatred against any identifiable group would not only be considered inappropriate, but could in fact lead to criminal charges."[38]

The incremental assault on free speech, through such mechanism as Section 13.1 of the Canadian Human Rights Act, that forbids any speech which *likely* might cause offense to people on the grounds of race, religion, gender or sexual orientation, has had an effect on public opinion in Canada. Senator Finley's effort in defending free speech was an indicator of this effect. But there were

---

[38] Steven Chase, "Ann Coulter's speech in Ottawa cancelled," *The Globe and Mail*, March 23, 2010.

other indicators that public opinion in the West was increasingly uneasy since 9/11 with multiculturalism as an ideology and official policy undermining the core liberal value of freedom based on individual rights and responsibilities.

Multiculturalism has meant immigrants are not required to assimilate into the host culture. In the years after 9/11, however, the public concern with erosion of free speech, fear of home grown terrorism, levels of immigration from non-Western cultures, and unemployment among newly arriving immigrants that strained the welfare benefits and social security arrangements in liberal democracies required of politicians to respond. But in liberal democracies elected politicians are generally followers, instead of makers and leaders of public opinion. Caution is a habit bred in successful politicians, of not being either too far ahead or too far behind the public on issues that might turn out to be of importance during elections. Reading the public mood is something of an art, and success in politics requires the art of gauging well the public mood and responding accordingly.

The response that startled Europe came from Germany's Chancellor Angela Merkel addressing a youth meeting of her ruling party, the Christian Democratic Union in October 2010. Merkel remarked, "At the start of the 60s we invited the guest-workers to Germany. We kidded ourselves for a while that they wouldn't stay, that one day they'd go home. That isn't what happened. And of course the tendency was to say: let's be 'multikulti' and live next to each other and enjoy being together, [but] this concept has failed, failed utterly."[39] Merkel's announcement on the failure of multiculturalism as an official policy was hugely important. Germany is the largest and richest member of the European Union, and given its history Germans have been guarded and reluctant in speaking about their unease with a policy that would brand them as bigots or worse.

But Merkel was not alone. A few months later in February 2011 Britain's Prime Minister David Cameron, speaking at a security conference in Munich, joined Merkel in declaring "multiculturalism has failed." He called for a stronger national identity and the need for

---

[39] Kate Connolly, "Angela Merkel declares death of German multiculturalism," *The Guardian*, October 17, 2010.

"more active, muscular liberalism."[40] Cameron's words were a useful reminder that liberalism is a fighting creed, and freedom cannot be taken for granted. In April 2011 France became the first European state to officially ban the "burka" — the veil worn by some Muslim women covering the entire face — in public.

The French measure could be viewed as somewhat of an extreme response directed at a very small number of Muslim women wearing the full veil in public, and infringing upon their liberty to dress as they please. But the dress code for women in Muslim countries under pressure from the fundamentalists, as in Saudi Arabia or Iran, had been politicized, and it indicated the public segregation of men and women in an Islamic society. The importation of such custom by Muslim immigrants to the West and its practice, however limited in numbers, also came to symbolize in the post-9/11 world a repudiation of liberal and secular values that had brought about the gains of the feminist movement. The French law against wearing "burka" indicated tolerance for those intolerant wilfully, or by custom, of liberal values had worn thin. Bernard-Henry Lévy, one of France's more visible public intellectuals, offered a strong and militant defence of the "burka" ban. He wrote:

This is not about the burka, it's about Voltaire. What is at stake is the Enlightenment of yesterday and today, and the heritage of both, no less sacred than that of the three monotheisms. A step backwards, just one, on this front would give the nod to all obscurantism, all fanaticism, all the true thoughts of hatred and violence.

And then, people finally say, "But what are we talking about here, anyway? How many cases? How many burkas? Why all this uproar for a few thousand, maybe just a few hundred, burkas to be found in the entirety of French territory, why dig up this arsenal of regulations, why pass a law?" That's the most popular argument at present and, for some, the most convincing. But in reality, it's as specious as all the others. For one of two things is true. Either it's just a game, an accoutrement, a costume, if you will, in which case tolerance would be the suitable response. Or else we're talking about an offence to women, a blow to their dignity, a blatant challenge to the fundamental republican rule of equality between the sexes. In that case, it is

---

[40] "State multiculturalism has failed, says Cameron," *BBC.co.uk*, February 5, 2011.

170

a question of principle. And when principles are involved, the numbers involved are of no consequence.[41]

In effect, the defence of republican principle and Enlightenment value by invoking Voltaire that Lévy offered was also logically a clear and straight-forward affirmation of the fundamental values of liberal democracy. Once we assert that individuals are free and equal irrespective of their ethnicity or beliefs, we then have arrived at the summit of political philosophy since Plato and Aristotle as to how society might arrange its legal and political order. From this summit of individual rights and freedoms, any so-called advance in the name of multiculturalism, ironically, can only mean going downward to an inferior or relatively degraded political arrangement.

Taken together the openly stated views of Germany's Chancellor Angela Merkel and Britain's Prime Minister David Cameron, the decision of the French government to legislate the banning of burka, and the acquittal by the Netherlands Court of Appeals of Geert Wilders of all charges of inciting hatred and discrimination against Muslims as a visible minority group, showed that despite nearly half-century of official multiculturalism the political philosophy of liberalism as the keystone principle of the modern West was not entirely eroded. At a minimum Britain, France and Germany together as the three largest members of the European Union let it be known that containment, or pushing back, of official multiculturalism needed to be publicly discussed.

IV.

An open society, liberal democracy, and the rule of law are not the natural state of man but historical achievements that have come about at great expense. Though their values are universal, they have been realized, if not in their entirety, at least in great measure only in the West against the indefatigable opposition of those who decry the role of reason over religious doctrines, loathe openness and freedom in

---

[41] Bernard-Henry Lévy, "In Voltaire's name, show your face," *National Post*, April 14, 2011.

favour of the closed circle of tribal and collectivist values, and denounce democracy as a recipe for anarchy. The enemies of open society are vast in number and, like tidal waves relentlessly beating down on dykes that, if not regularly attended, would break and be washed away, they remain unforgiving and tireless in their effort to wreck the open society and freedoms that distinguish liberal democracy from any other form of political arrangement in the history of man and society.

The first and most important line of defence of freedom as the foundation for the open society and liberal democracy on which rest the historical achievements of the West is education. It means first learning and then being repeatedly reminded of how Canada's founding values are those of the open society and liberal democracy. In *Fearful Symmetry: The Fall and Rise of Canada's Founding Values* Brian Lee Crowley writes, "Central to this view of the character of Canadians and their institutions was a notion of individual freedom and responsibility, a belief that each of us was endowed with a nature that required us to be responsible and accountable for our choices. The corollary was that if we deprived men and women of their freedom and responsibility for themselves, we prevented people from being fully free and fully human" (2009: 44). Crowley cites as a reminder the inspirational words of Richard Cartwright, spoken in the legislature of the United Province of Canada in 1865: "I think every true reformer, every real friend of liberty, will agree with me in saying that if we must erect safeguards, they should be rather for the security of the individual than of the mass, and that our chiefest care must be to train the majority to respect the rights of the minority, to prevent the claims of the few from being trampled underfoot by the caprice or passion of the many. For myself, sir, I own frankly I prefer British liberty to American equality" (ibid: 45).

There is in Cartwright's speech a resounding echo of Mill's liberalism and Tocqueville's concern over the tyranny of the majority; and there is the clarity of understanding that the strength of a liberal democracy comes from its unbending defence of freedom in which the "security of the individual" — the ultimate minority of one against a majority that can turn into a mob — is its defining virtue as the good society. This understanding of why a liberal democracy cannot be improved on by the flawed logic of multiculturalism needs to be *rediscovered*, *restated* and *reaffirmed* without apology or equivocation if freedom and democracy are to remain secure against the scheming of their enemies.

Finally, and one more time, it needs stating that the worm inside the doctrine of multiculturalism is the lie that all cultures are worthy of equal respect and equally embracing of individual freedom and democracy. The concerted assault by the Islamists on the essential and life-affirming values based on individual rights and freedoms is proof of this lie. A large portion of the world's population, quite likely the majority, at the beginning of the twenty-first century live under some sort of authoritarianism of one-party rule headed by leaders without humour or any other redeeming qualities, such as kindness, humility, intelligence, wit, that free people instinctively recognize and respect. A liberal democracy, such as Canada, is inherently open and accepting of the other, and whenever and wherever there is an impediment to such acceptance it can be met with and overcome through reasoning and dialogue. There is, moreover, in a liberal democracy no basis for ethnocentric prejudice by the majority population to reject the cultural norms of ethnic minorities. But when any aspect of such cultural norms collides with the core values of a liberal democracy, then that aspect needs to be reformed or rejected accordingly. In order for this to occur, for any reasonable accommodation to work in an ethnically diverse Canada, there needs to be a clear understanding without any ambiguity among all Canadians, irrespective of their ethnicity, that there is a unifying Canadian culture deeply embedded in the values of the West and shaped by the Enlightenment. This Canadian culture is open and inclusive, embracing of others, tolerant and generous, and deserving of the unapologetic support of all who cherish freedom as God's most precious gift.

References

Abella, I. M. and Harold Troper. 1982. *None is too many: Canada and the Jews of Europe, 1933-1948*. Toronto: Lester & Orpen Dennys.

Ahmed, L. 1992. *Women and Gender in Islam: Historical Roots of a Modern Debate*. New Haven & London: Yale University Press.

Akhtar, S. 1989. *Be Careful With Muhammad! The Salman Rushdie Affair*. London: Bellew Publishing.

Algar, H. 2002. *Wahhabism: A Critical Essay*. Oneonta, New York: Islamic Publications International.

Allen, C. 2006. *God's Terrorists The Wahhabi Cult and the Hidden Roots of Modern Jihad*. London: Little, Brown.

Alexiev, A. 2003. "Wahhabism: State-Sponsored Extremism World Wide." Testimony Before the U.S. Senate Subcommittee on Terrorism, Technology, and Homeland Security, June 26. (http://kyl.senate.gov/legis_center/subdocs/sco62603_alexiev.pdf)

Anderson, B. 1991. *Imagined Communities*, revised edition. London: Verso.

Archbishop's Lecture, 2008. *Civil and Religious Law in England: a Religious Perspective*. February 7. Available online: (www.archbishopofcanterbury.org/1575).

Aristotle. 1943. *Politics* in the Collected Work of Aristotle, *On Man In The Universe*. New York: Walter J. Black, Inc.

Aron, R. 1968. *Main Currents in Sociological Thought*. Volume I. New York: Doubleday & Company.

Barber, B.R. 1996. *Jihad Vs. McWorld: How Globalism and Tribalism Are Reshaping The World*. New York: Ballantine Books.

Barker, E. 1960. *Social Contract: Essays by Locke, Hume, and Rousseau*. Oxford: Oxford University Press.

Bauman, Z. 2004. *Identity*. London: Polity Press.

Bawer, B. 2009. *Surrender: Appeasing Islam, Sacrificing Freedom*. New York: Doubleday.

Bell, S. 2005. *Cold Terror: How Canada Nurtures and Exports Terrorism Around the World*. Mississauga, ON: Wiley (Canada).

Bellamy, R. 2008. *Citizenship: A Very Short Introduction*. New York: Oxford University Press.

Berlin, I. 1969. "Two Concepts of Liberty," in *Four Essays On Liberty*. Oxford: Oxford University Press.

Bissett, J. 2009. "The current state of Canadian immigration policy," in H. Grubel (ed.), *The Effects of Mass Immigration on Canadian Living Standards and Society*. Vancouver: Fraser Institute.

Bissoondath, N. 1994. *Selling Illusions: The Cult of Multiculturalism in Canada*. Toronto: Penguin Books.

Bloom, A. 1987. *The Closing of the American Mind*. New York: Simon & Schuster.

Bolan, K. 2005. *Loss of Faith: How the Air-India Bombers Got Away With Murder*. Toronto: McClelland & Stewart.

Bouchard, G. and C. Taylor, 2008. *Building the Future: A Time for Reconciliation* (Abridged Report). Gouvernement du Quebec.

Brody, B.A. 1980. *Identity and Essence*. Princeton, NJ: Princeton University Press.

Bruckner, P. 2010. *The Tyranny of Guilt: An Essay on Western Masochism*. Princeton, NJ: Princeton University Press.

Bruckner, P. 1986. *The Tears of White Man: Compassion as Contempt*. New York: The Free Press.

Burckhardt, J. 1979. *Reflections on History*. Indianapolis: Liberty Classics.

Buruma, I. 2006. *Murder in Amsterdam: The Death of Theo van Gogh and the Limits of Tolerance*. New York: Penguin.

Calhoun, C. 1997. *Nationalism*. Minneapolis: University of Minnesota Press.

Caldwell, C. 2009. *Reflections On The Revolution In Europe: Immigration, Islam, And The West*. New York: Doubleday.

Cassirer, E. 1951. *The Philosophy of the Enlightenment*. Princeton, NJ: Princeton University Press.

Cassirer, E. 1944. *An Essay On Man: An Introduction to a Philosophy of Human Culture*. New Haven and London: Yale University Press.

Chadwick, O. 1975. *The Secularization of the European Mind*.

Cambridge, UK: Cambridge University Press.

Charfi, M. 2005. *Islam and Liberty: The Historical Misunderstanding.* London & New York: Zed Books.

Chiaromonte, N. 1985. *The Paradox of History.* Philadelphia: University of Pennsylvania Press.

Chomsky, N. 1993. *Year 501: The Conquest Continues.* Montreal/New York: Black Rose Books.

Clarkson, S. and Christina McCall. 1991. *Trudeau and Our Times: The Magnificent Obsession* (volume 1). Toronto: McClelland & Stewart.

Cohen, A. 2007. *The Unfinished Canadian: The People We Are.* Toronto: McClelland & Stewart.

Coulson, N.J. 1964. *A History of Islamic Law.* Edinburgh: Edinburgh University Press.

Crowley, B.E. 2009. *Fearful Symmetry: The Fall and Rise of Canada's Founding Values.* Toronto: Key Porter Books.

Dacey, A. 2008. *The Secular Conscience: Why Belief Belongs in Public Life.* Amherst, NY: Prometheus Books.

Dalrymple, T. 2008. *Not With A Bang But A Whimper: The Politics and Culture of Decline.* Chicago: Ivan R. Dee.

Dunn, J. 2005. *Democracy: A History.* Toronto: Penguin.

Dunn, J. 2003. *Locke: A Very Short Introduction.* New York: Oxford University Press.

Easterly, W. 2006. *The White Man's Burden.* New York: Penguin Books.

Ehrenfeld, R. 2005. *Funding Evil: How Terrorism Is Financed and How To Stop It.* New York: Bonus Books.

El Saadawi, N. 1980. *The Hidden Face of Eve: Women in the Arab World.* London: Zed Press.

Flexner, E. 1975. *Century of struggle: the woman's rights movement in the United States.* Cambridge, MA: Harvard University Press.

Friesen, J. 1997. *Rediscovering the First Nations of Canada.* Calgary: Detselig Enterprises Ltd.

Frye, N. 1991. *The Modern Century: The Whidden Lectures 1967.* Toronto: Oxford University Press.

Gairdner, W.D. 2010. *The Trouble with Canada...Still! A Citizen Speaks Out.* Toronto: Key Porter Books.

Gairdner, W.D. 1990. *The Trouble with Canada: A Citizen Speaks*

Out. Toronto: Stoddart.

Geertz, C. 1973. *The Interpretation of Cultures*. New York: Basic Books.

Geertz, C. ed. 1963. *Old Societies and New States: The Quest for Modernity in Asia and Africa*. New York: Free Press.

Gellner, E. 1983. *Nations and Nationalism*. Ithaca, NY: Cornell University Press.

Gerth, H.H. and C. Wright Mills (editors). 1946. *From Max Weber: Essays in Sociology*. New York: Oxford University Press.

Granatstein, J.L. 1998. *Who Killed Canadian History?* Toronto: HarperCollins.

Grant, G. P. 1982. *Lament for a Nation: The Defeat of Canadian Nationalism*. Ottawa: Carleton University Press.

Gray, J. 1995. *Liberalism*. Second Edition. Minneapolis: University of Minnesota Press.

Griffiths, R. 2009. *Who We Are: A Citizen's Manifesto*. Vancouver and Toronto: Douglas & McIntyre.

Gwyn, R. 1980. *The Northern Magus: Pierre Trudeau and Canadians*. Toronto: McClelland & Stewart.

Habeck, M.R. 2006. *Knowing the Enemy: Jihadist Ideology and the War on Terror*. New Haven & London: Yale University Press.

Hall, J. A. and G. John Ikenberry. 1989. *The State*. Minneapolis: University of Minnesota Press.

Hallaq, W.B. 2009. *Shari`a: Theory, Practice, Transformations*. New York: Cambridge University Press.

Hansard (Official Report). 2010. *Debates of the Senate*. 3rd Session, 40th Parliament, Vol. 147, Issue 13. Canadian Government Publishing Centre, Ottawa.

Hansard (Official Report). 1988. *Debates of the Senate*. 2nd Session, 33rd Parliament, Vol. 131, Number 132. Canadian Government Publishing Centre, Ottawa.

Hawkins, F. 1988. *Canada and Immigration: Public Policy and Public Concern*. Second Edition. Kingston and Montreal: McGill-Queen's University Press.

Hayek, F.A. 1992. *The Fortunes of Liberalism*, vol. 4, *Collected Works*. London: Routledge.

Hayek, F.A. 1960, reprint 2006. *The Constitution of Liberty*. London and New York: Routledge Classics.

Heater, D. 1990. *Citizenship: The Civic Ideal in World History,*

Politics and Education. London and New York: Longman.

Heilbroner, R.L. 1999. *The Worldly Philosophers: The Lives, Times, and Ideas of the Great Economic Thinkers* (Revised Seventh Edition). New York: Simon & Schuster.

Himmelfarb, G. 1974. "Editor's Introduction" in J.S. Mill, *On Liberty*. London: Penguin Books.

Hobsbawm, E. 1995. *Age of Extremes: The Short Twentieth Century 1914-1991*. London: Abacus.

Hobsbawm, E. 1990. *Nations and Nationalism Since 1780: Programme, Myth, Reality*. Cambridge, UK: Cambridge University Press.

Huntington, S.P. 2004. *Who Are We? The Challenges to America's National Identity*. New York: Simon & Schuster.

Huntington, S. P. 1996. *The Clash of Civilizations: Remaking of World Order*. New York: Simon & Schuster (Touchstone Book 1997).

Husain, E. 2007. *The Islamist*. London: Penguin Books.

Ibbitson, J. 2005. *The Polite Revolution: Perfecting the Canadian Dream*. Toronto: McClelland & Stewart.

Ibn Warraq. 2007. *Defending the West: A Critique of Edward Said's Orientalism*. New York: Prometheus Books.

Ignatieff, M. 1987. *The Russian Album*. New York: Viking Penguin.

Johnston, H. 1979. *The Voyage of the Komagata Maru: The Sikh Challenge to Canada's Colour Bar*. Delhi: Oxford University Press.

Kateb, G. 1992. *The Inner Ocean: Individualism and Democratic Culture*. Ithaca: Cornell University Press.

Kedourie, E. 1990. *Nationalism*, 4th edition. Oxford: Blackwell (first Published 1960).

Kennedy, J.F. 1964. *A Nations of Immigrants*. Revised and Enlarged Edition. Toronto: Popular Library.

Khalidi, R. 2004. *Resurrecting Empire: Western Footprints and America's Perilous Path in the Middle East*. Boston: Beacon Press.

Koestler, A. 1964. *Darkness at Noon*. London: Penguin.

Koser, K. 2007. *International Migration: A Very Short Introduction*. New York: Oxford University Press.

Kukathas, C. 2003. *The Liberal Archipelago: A Theory of Diversity and Freedom*. Oxford: Oxford University Press.

Kymlicka, W. 2007. *Multicultural Odysseys: Navigating the New International Politics of Diversity*. Oxford: Oxford University Press.

Kymlicka, W. 2004. "Canadian Multiculturalism in Historical and Comparative Perspective," in M. Zachariah, A. Sheppard, L. Barratt (editors), *Canadian Multiculturalism: Dreams, Realities, Expectations*. Edmonton, AL: Canadian Multicultural Education Foundation.

Kymlicka, W. 1995. *Multicultural Citizenship: A Liberal Theory of Minority Rights*. Oxford: Oxford University Press.

Lal, D. 2004. *In Praise of Empires: Globalization and Order*. New York: Palgrave Macmillan.

Levant, E. 2009. *Shakedown: How Our Government Is Undermining Democracy in the Name of Human Rights*. Toronto: McClelland & Stewart.

Lewis, A. 2007. *Freedom for the Thought That We Hate: A Biography of the First Amendment*. New York: Basic Books.

Lloyd, T.O. 1971. *Suffragettes International: the world-wide campaign for women's rights*. New York: American Heritage Press.

Lovejoy, A.O. 1964. *The Great Chain of Being*. Cambridge, Mass.: Harvard University Press.

Lukacs, J. 1985. *Historical Consciousness or the Remembered Past*. New York: Schocken Books.

Maalouf, A. 2001. *In the Name of Identity*. New York: Arcade Publishing.

MacIntyre, A. 1981. *After Virtue*. Indiana: University of Notre Dame Press.

MacLennan, H. 1945. *Two Solitudes*. Toronto: Collins.

MacMillan, M. 2009. *The Uses and Abuses of History*. Toronto: Penguin Canada.

Macpherson, C.B. 1965. *The Real World of Democracy*. The Massey Lectures. Toronto: CBC Enterprises/les Enterprises Radio-Canada (Sixteenth printing 1987).

Mansur, S. 2009. *Islam's Predicament: Perspectives of a Dissident Muslim*. Oakville, Canada: Mosaic Press.

McLachlin, B. 2004. "Protecting Constitutional Rights: A Comparative View of the United States and Canada." Ottawa: Supreme Court of Canada.

McNaught, K. 1969. *The Pelican History of Canada*. London: Penguin Books.

McWhirter, D.A. 1994. *Freedom of Speech, Press, and Assembly*. Phoenix, Arizona: The Oryx Press.

Mernissi, F. 1991. *The Veil and the Male Elite: A Feminist Interpretation of Women's Right in Islam*. New York: Addison-Wesley.

Mill, J.S. 1991. *On Liberty and Other Essays*. New York: Oxford University Press.

Mill, J.S. 1974. *On Liberty*. London: Penguin Books.

Milton, J. 1898. *Areopagitica*. Edited with introduction and notes by John W. Hales. Oxford: Clarendon Press.

Miri, M. 2003. *Identity and Moral Life*. New Delhi: Oxford University Press.

Modood, T. 2007. *Multiculturalism: A Civic Idea*. Cambridge, UK: Polity Press.

Moon, R. 2008. *Report to the Canadian Human Rights Commission Concerning Section 13 of the Canadian Human Rights Act and the Regulation of Hate Speech on the Internet*. Ottawa: Canadian Human Rights Commission.

Morton, D. 2000. "Strains of Affluence," in Craig Brown (ed), *The Illustrated History of Canada*, pp. 469-570. Toronto: Key Porter Books.

Moyo, D. 2009. *Dead Aid: Why Aid Is Not Working And How There Is A Better Way For Africa*. New York: Farrar, Straus and Giroux.

National Commission, 2004. *The 9/11 Commission Report*. New York: W.W. Norton (Authorized Edition).

Neusner, J. 1989. *Who, Where and What is "Israel"?* Lanham, MD: University Press of America.

Nozick, R. 1974. *Anarchy, State and Utopia*. Oxford: Blackwell.

Palmer, H. ed. 1975. *Immigration and the Rise of Multiculturalism*. Toronto: Copp Clark Publishing.

Parekh, B. 2000. *Rethinking Multiculturalism: Cultural Diversity and Political Theory*. London: Macmillan Press.

Pew Research Center. 2009a. *Mapping the Global Muslim Population*. October (www.pewresearch.org).

Pew Research Center. 2009b. *Muslims Widely Seen As Facing Discrimination*. September 9 (www.pewresearch.org).

Phillips, M. 2006. *Londonistan*. New York: Encounter Books.

Pipes, D. 2003. *The Rushdie Affair: The Novel, the Ayatollah, and the West*. New Brunswick, NJ: Transaction Publishers; Second Edition.

Plato. 1965. *Timaeus and Critias*. London: Penguin.

Popper, K.S. 1971. *The Open Society and Its Enemies. Volume I. The Spell of Plato*. Princeton, NJ.: Princeton University Press.

Powell, E.J. 1991. *Reflections of a Statesman: The Writings and Speeches of Enoch Powell*. London: Bellew.

Rashid, A. 2001. *Taliban: Militant Islam, Oil & Fundamentalism in Central Asia*. New Haven & London: Yale University Press.

Rawls, J. 1993. *Political Liberalism*. New York: Columbia University Press.

Rawls, J. 1971. *A Theory of Justice*. Cambridge, Mass.: Harvard University Press.

Revel, J.F. 1983. *How Democracies Perish*. New York: Doubleday.

Roy, P. E. 2003. *The Oriental Question: Consolidating a White Man's Province, 1914-41*. Vancouver: University of British Columbia Press.

Royal Commission. 1965. *A preliminary report of the Royal Commission on Bilingualism and Biculturalism*. Ottawa: Queen's Printer and Controller of Stationery.

Rushdie, S. 1992. *Imaginary Homelands: Essays and Criticism 1981-1991*. London: Penguin Books.

Ruthven, M. 2002. *A Fury For God: The Islamist Attack on America*. London: Granta Books.

Ruthven, M. 1990. *A Satanic Affair: Salman Rushdie & The Rage of Islam*. London: Chatto & Windus.

Said, E. 1979. *Orientalism*. New York: Vintage Books.

Schlesinger, A.M. 1998. *The Disuniting of America: Reflections on a Multicultural Society*. Revised and Enlarged Edition. New York: W.W. Norton.

Schwartz, S. 2002. *The Two Faces of Islam: The House of Sa'ud From Tradition To Terror*. New York: Doubleday.

Scruton, R. 2002. *The West and the Rest: Globalization and the Terrorist Threat*. Wilmington, DE: ISI Books.

Sen, A. 2006. *Identity and Violence: The Illusion of Destiny*. New York and London: W.W. Norton & Company.

Shoemaker, S. 1963. *Self-Knowledge and Self-Identity*. Ithaca, NY:

Cornell University Press.

Smith, A. 1991. *National Identity*. London: Penguin.

Statistics Canada. 2003. *2001 Census: analysis series. Canada's ethnocultural portrait: The changing mosaic*. Ottawa.

Talisse, R.B. 2001. *On Rawls: A Liberal Theory of Justice and Justification*. Belmont, CA: Wadsworth/Thomson Learning, Inc.

Taylor, A.J.P. 1965. *English History 1914-1945*. Oxford: Oxford University Press.

Taylor, C. 1992. *Multiculturalism and "The Politics of Recognition"*. With commentary by Amy Guttman (Editor), Steven C. Rockefeller, Michael Walzer, Susan Wolfe. Princeton, NJ: Princeton University Press.

Thucydides. 1954. *The Peloponnesian War*. London: Penguin.

Tocqueville, A. 2000. *Democracy in America*. Translated, Edited and with an Introduction by Harvey C. Mansfield and Debra Winthrop. Chicago: The University of Chicago Press.

Toffler, A. 1970. *Future Shock*. New York: Random House.

Trigger, B. 1985. *Natives and Newcomers: Canada's Heroic Age Reconsidered*. Montreal: McGill-Queen's University Press.

United Nations Development Programme (UNDP). 2002. *Arab Human Development Report 2002: Creating Opportunities for Future Generations*. New York: UN Publications.

Ward, W. P. 1990. *White Canada Forever: Popular Attitudes and Public Policy Toward Orientals in British Columbia* (second edition). Montreal: McGill-Queen's University Press.

Williamson, J.G. 2005. *The Political Economy of World Mass Migration: Comparing Two Global Centuries*. Washington, D.C.: The AEI Press.

Young, M. 1998. "Canadian Citizenship Act And Current Issues." Ottawa: Depository Services Program, Government of Canada.

ACKNOWLEDGEMENTS

This project on multiculturalism was initially commissioned by the Atlantic Institute of Market Studies (AIMS) in Halifax, Nova Scotia, and I want to thank Brian Crowley, its former president, Charles Cirtwill, its current president, and Barbara Pike, Ian Munro, Bobby O'Keefe and Lori Peddle for their kindness, patience, and support through the preparation and writing of it, and Barry Norris for editorial help. I want to thank my publisher Howard Rotberg for bringing out this book, and a number of friends with whom I discussed the subject. I am indebted to Reuben Bromstein and William Gairdner for their friendship, and for sharing their thoughts with me on reading drafts of this work in earlier stages of writing; to Naresh Raghubeer, David Harris and Marc Lebuis for their support whenever I needed any assistance; to Munawar Karim and Joydeep Mukherji for the many long and pleasant hours we have spent together over many years discussing history and politics; to Robert Addington, Mary Lou Ambrogio, Bessie and David Borwein, Susan Cassan, Chris Essex, Rory Leishman, John Palmer, Alan Perlmutter, Rénald Richler, and Eva Ryten in our Saturday morning Starbucks club for their interest in my work and for readily sharing with me their thoughts while discussing the subject over many wonderful cups of coffee; to my wife, Yasmina, without her kindness and love I would not be able to work with the ease I do; to my daughter Ines, and my son Samir, who give me the joy and purpose of living; and, I mention him last only because he has been so special during the period I worked on this study, to Ben Singer, a respected colleague at the University of Western Ontario and a dear friend, to whom I dedicate this study in gratitude for the sort of support he has always extended to me. It is needless to state that without the help and personal kindness of friends mentioned, and many who remain unmentioned, completing this work would have been tedious. I am, however, solely responsible for this study, the arguments made, the conclusion reached, and any flaw that discerning readers may find.